DAILY PRAYERS
FOR THE
PEOPLE OF GOD

DAILY PRAYERS
FOR THE
PEOPLE OF GOD

Owen O'Sullivan

BOOKS & MEDIA
BOSTON

First published in Great Britain in 2001 by
SPCK
Holy Trinity Church
Marylebone Road
London NW1 4DU

Imprimi Potest: Dermot Lynch, February 22, 2000

Nihil Obstat: Rev. John McEvoy, February 14, 2000

Imprimatur: Laurence Ryan DD, Bishop of Kildare and Leighlin,
February 22, 2000

British Library Cataloguing-in-Publication Data
A catalogue record for this book is available from the British Library

Unless otherwise noted, the scripture quotations contained herein
are from the *New Revised Standard Version Bible: Catholic Edition*,
copyright 1989 by the Division of Christian Education of the National
Council of the Churches of Christ in the U.S.A. Used by permission.
All rights reserved.

Typeset by Pioneer Associates, Perthshire
Printed in Great Britain by
Omnia Books, Glasgow

ISBN 0-8198-1879-8

Published in the U.S.A. by Pauline Books & Media,
50 St. Paul's Avenue, Boston, MA 02130-3491.

http://www.pauline.org

Pauline Books & Media is the publishing house of the Daughters of
St. Paul, an international congregation of women religious serving the
Church with the communications media.
1 2 3 4 5 6 7 8 9 07 06 05 04 03 02 01

CONTENTS

*This book is dedicated to
my brother Vincent,
his wife Veronica
and their children,
John and Clare.*

PREFACE

'The Spirit helps us in our weakness; for we do not know how to pray as we ought, but that very Spirit intercedes with sighs too deep for words. And God, who searches the heart, knows what is the mind of the Spirit, because the Spirit intercedes for the saints according to the will of God' (*Romans 8.26–27*). Anyone who has ever seriously tried to pray knows how true it is to say, 'We do not know how to pray as we ought'. But prayer is less a matter of what *we* do, or even try to do, than of what God does in us, if we create a space: 'If at first the "I" seems to be the most important element in prayer, prayer teaches us that the situation is actually different. The "Thou" is more important because our prayer begins with God . . . it is always God's initiative within us.'[1]

This book is for ordinary men and women, and takes their working week into consideration. For instance, Sunday is a day of community prayer for most Christians, centring on the Eucharist; the prayers chosen for Sunday reflect this. Similarly, Monday is the start of the working week, so the prayers are often directed to the theme of work and commitment to service. Those during the week recall the ordinary challenges and demands of working life: good relationships with others, social justice, discernment, speaking the truth with justice and kindness, deliverance from temptation, trusting in Providence, and seeking forgiveness – among many others. Constant themes throughout the entire week are those of thanksgiving, celebration and praise of God. In keeping with a long-standing Christian tradition, Friday is a day of reflection on the suffering and death of Christ; prayers for that day focus on people's tiredness from work, the need for perseverance and forgiveness of sin, prayer for the sick, the dying and the dead, and the search for meaning in suffering. Saturday is a day, if not of rest, then at least of change from ordinary work, and ideally a family day; the prayers chosen respond to this need. Saturday evening prayers are often a preparation for the Sunday Eucharist. As weekends are less pressured in terms of demands on time, prayers and reflections for Saturday and Sunday are usually a little longer than for other days.

If you can't say a prayer for yourself, e.g. one for the sick if you're well (or one for the dead!) you can always say it for another. A Christian's prayer is never a solo, do-it-yourself effort; even when said alone, it is always with others, for others, and in the name of others. In order to emphasize this community dimension, some prayers have been adapted from the original by changing them from the singular to the plural. However, prayers of confession of sin are always in the singular: our personal sins are solely our own responsibility.

One way of using the book is to read some or all of the prayers for each period, and to consider one of the Reflections. Continue in this way until the weeks have been completed; then start again, taking for consideration a different Reflection, and so on. (Where possible, Reflections have been chosen which resonate with the prayers.) The weeks given in the book are not related to the liturgical year, they stand independently of it.

It is best to read slowly and reflectively, with frequent periods of silence, allowing the meaning to sink in and take hold. It is better to say one prayer thoughtfully than to feel under pressure to say them all in order to 'get them in'. It is not important to finish a page in each period of prayer; what matters is to pray well, keeping in mind that 'the best kind of prayer is that in which there is most love'. What matters is for prayer to be genuine and from the heart: 'What the mouth speaks, let the mind within confess; what the tongue utters, let the heart feel.'[2]

The user should feel free to adapt the prayers to his or her situation by, for example, changing the number or person of a phrase, or by adding personal favourites. In a similar vein, many have been amended to make them inclusive of women and men. Where a prayer or reflection has been adapted for any reason, this is indicated in the reference which follows.

The style of the book makes it most suitable for private use, as that involves least adaptation. (Its content is of value, I hope, in public as well as in private.) For communal use, it offers much, provided that the prayer leader is willing to give a little time to preparation and adaptation, and to communicate clearly with the group. Flexibility finds a way around most problems: 'I think it useful to have diversity and variety in the prayers and psalms at the regular hours, because, where there is monotony, the soul tends to become weary and distracted: but when there is change and variety in the psalmody and in the pattern of each hour, then the desire of the soul is renewed and concentration is restored.'[3]

The sources on which I have drawn in compiling this book are as follows:

The Bible: I have drawn especially on the Psalms, from which there are some twenty extracts. Other prayers and canticles of both Testaments, as well as short phrases or aspirations, have been used, sometimes with substantial adaptation, such as by linking phrases from different parts of a text.

The liturgy: In the words of Pope Paul VI, the liturgy is 'an incomparable school of spirituality'.[4] Where liturgical prayer and private prayer are integrated, each drawing on the other for support, they strengthen and enrich each other, and give a unity and wholeness to the spirituality of an individual or community. I have used especially missals and sacramentaries, breviaries, rituals and benedictionals, both ancient and modern.

The Fathers of the Church: They provide an almost limitless resource, though a good deal of editorial work is necessary to make them more resonant with contemporary sensibilities and priorities. Sometimes texts from different parts of a writer's work have been drawn together into one: an example of this is the conflation of extracts from the *Confessions* of Saint Augustine.

Ecumenical: Prayers have been drawn from Catholic, Anglican, Orthodox and Protestant sources, as also from Celtic spirituality, the latter experiencing something of a renaissance in recent years, and now deservedly enjoying its place in the sun. Its gutsy, down-to-earth style, in tune with nature and constantly evoking powerful mental images that are fresh and appealing, resonate well with our contemporaries. For all its appeal, it does not lack challenge, especially regarding the care of the poor.

Apart from a few quotations from Jewish sources – and the Jews are our older brothers and sisters in the faith – I have not quoted non-Christian prayers. This is not because I think them unsuitable – quite the contrary, in fact: as Ambrosiaster wrote, 'All truth is God's truth, by whomsoever it is mediated.'[5] But I feel that to do so might be considered by some non-Christians as a covert attempt to 'co-opt' their thoughts and ideas to ours, and might therefore be resented by them. In addition, because of my unfamiliarity with non-Christian religion in general and prayer in particular, I do not feel competent to use their prayers without the risk of wrenching them out of their context and injecting into them a meaning which might not be that of the original writers, and that would be to do them an injustice. A book of prayers from all religions, including so-called 'pagan' religions, such as those of the original peoples of North America or Africa, is an attractive project, but it calls for a competence greater than mine: 'Wherever people are praying in the world, there the Holy Spirit is, the living breath of prayer.'[6]

There are not many quotations from contemporary writers of prayers. I find that a mixture of old and new is a difficult blend to bring together satisfactorily without an excess of changes of mood and context, without jarring and jolting from one frame of mind to another. It is analogous to the problem of renovating an old church building: it is often best to leave it in its original style than try to modernize it, ending up with the church of 'Saint Formica'. Choosing between the old and the new in prayers, I opted for the old.

A limitation in the book is the relative scarcity of prayers for married people, families, children and healing, or prayers about work and social responsibility. These are difficult to find in the traditional sources on which I drew, though I tried to make the best use of what was there by drawing, for example, on Anglican sources, which have a good deal to offer in those areas. The reason for this limitation is that many traditional prayers derive from a monastic spirituality. One of the benefits of developments in recent years is that modern writers of liturgical texts and private prayers are well aware of this limitation and give such prayers greater representation than in the past. In a similar way, prayers by women, which were almost non-existent in earlier years, are now widely available.

The best way to learn how to pray is to start doing it. Like swimming, you have to take the plunge and get into it; sitting on a river bank reading a book on how to swim is not enough. The way to do it is to do it, and the way to do it better is to do it more often. Dom John Chapman summarizes it well: 'Pray as you can, and don't try to pray as you can't.'[7]

Notes

1. Pope John Paul II, *Crossing the Threshold of Hope*, ed. by Vittorio Messori, Jonathan Cape, London, 1994, pp. 16, 17.
2. Saint Ambrose, *On the Mysteries*, nn. 52–54.
3. Saint Basil of Caesarea, *Extended Monastic Rule*, n. 37.
4. Pope Paul VI, *Ecclesiam Suam*, n. 38.
5. Ambrosiaster, *Patrologia Latina* 17, 245.
6. Pope John Paul II, *Dominum et Vivificantem*, n. 65.
7. Dom John Chapman, *Spiritual Letters*, Sheed and Ward, London, 1935, p. 25.

⋘ *Daily Prayers* ⋙

In the name of the Father, and of the Son, and of the Holy Spirit. Amen.

The Lord's Prayer

Our Father, who art in heaven, hallowed be thy name; thy kingdom come; thy will be done on earth as it is in heaven. Give us this day our daily bread, and forgive us our trespasses as we forgive those who trespass against us; and lead us not into temptation but deliver us from evil.

(See Matthew 6.9–13; Luke 11.2–4).

Soul of Christ

Soul of Christ, sanctify me.
Body of Christ, heal me.
Blood of Christ, drench me.
Water from the side of Christ, wash me.
Passion of Christ, strengthen me.
Good Jesus, hear me.
In your wounds, shelter me.
From turning away, keep me.
From the evil one, protect me.
At the hour of my death, call me.
Into your presence, lead me,
to praise you with all your saints
for ever and ever. Amen.

(Anon, fourteenth century)

Look kindly on your church

God of power and eternal light, look kindly on your church, that wonderful and sacred mystery; and, by your constant care, carry out the task of your people's salvation. Let the whole world feel and see that things which were cast down are being raised up, that those which had grown old are being made new, and that all things are returning to perfection, through him from whom they started, Jesus Christ, your Son, our Lord. Amen.

(Gelasian Sacramentary)

Bless all Christian families

Bless all Christian families, especially (*names*). May the light of your presence shine in them and from them to the world. Amen.

(Adapted from the Catholic Truth Society)

* * *

Reflections

Love the Bible and wisdom will love you; love it and it will preserve you; honour it and it will embrace you.

(Saint Jerome)

Praise to the Lord for he is good, for his steadfast love endures for ever.

(2 Chronicles 5.13)

The family is the domestic church.

(Vatican II, Lumen Gentium)

There is no other God

There is no other God,
there never was and there never will be,
than God the Father
unbegotten and without beginning,
from whom is all beginning,
the Lord of the universe as we have been taught;
and his son Jesus Christ
whom we declare to have always been with the Father
and to have been begotten spiritually by the Father
before the beginning of the world,
before all beginning,
in a way that defies description;
and by him are made all things, visible and invisible.
He was made man,
defeated death,
and was received into heaven by the Father,
who has given him power over all names
in heaven, on earth, and under the earth;
and every tongue will acknowledge to him
that Jesus Christ is the Lord God.
We believe in him
and we look for his coming soon
as judge of the living and the dead,
who will treat all according to their deeds.
He has poured out the Holy Spirit on us in abundance,
the gift and the guarantee of eternal life,
who makes those who believe and obey
children of God and joint heirs with Christ.
We acknowledge and adore him
as one God in the Trinity of the holy name.

(Attributed to Saint Patrick)

Blessing

May the love of the Lord Jesus draw us to himself;
may the power of the Lord Jesus strengthen us in his service;
may the joy of the Lord Jesus fill our souls.
May the blessing of God almighty, Father, Son, and Holy Spirit
be among us and remain with us always. Amen.

(William Temple)

* * *

Reflections

The Old Testament proclaimed the Father clearly, but the Son
more obscurely. The New Testament revealed the Son, and gave
us a glimpse of the divinity of the Spirit. Now the Spirit dwells
among us and grants us a clearer vision of himself.

(Saint Gregory Nazianzus)

Keep silent! – What a strange expression! Silence keeps us.

(Georges Bernanos)

If you had walked in the way of God, you would be living in
peace forever. Learn where there is wisdom, where there is
strength, where there is understanding, so that you may at the
same time discern where there is length of days, and life, where
there is light for the eyes, and peace.

(Baruch 3.13–14)

Paraphrase of the Lord's Prayer

Our Father: Most holy, our Creator and Redeemer, our Saviour and our Comforter.

Who art in heaven: In the angels and the saints. You give them light so that they may have knowledge, because you, Lord, are light. You inflame them so that they may have love, because you, Lord, are love. You live continually in them and you fill them so that they may be happy, because you, Lord, are the supreme good, the eternal good, and it is from you all good comes, and without you there is no good.

Hallowed be thy name: May our knowledge of you become ever clearer, so that we may realize the extent of your benefits, the steadfastness of your promises, the sublimity of your majesty and the depth of your judgements.

Thy kingdom come: So that you may reign in us by your grace and bring us to your kingdom, where we shall see you clearly, love you perfectly, be happy in your company and enjoy you for ever.

Thy will be done on earth as it is in heaven: That we may love you with our whole heart by always thinking of you; with our whole mind by directing our whole intention towards you and seeking your glory in everything; and with all our strength by spending all our energies and affections of soul and body in the service of your love alone. And may we love our neighbours as ourselves, encouraging all to love you as best we can, rejoicing at the good fortune of others, just as if it were our own, and sympathizing with their misfortunes, while giving offence to no one.

Give us this day our daily bread: Your own beloved Son, our Lord Jesus Christ, to remind us of the love he showed for us and to help us understand and appreciate it and everything that he did or said or suffered.

And forgive us our trespasses: In your infinite mercy, and by the power of the passion of your Son, our Lord Jesus Christ, together with the merits and the intercession of the Blessed Virgin Mary and all your saints.

As we forgive those who trespass against us: And if we do not forgive perfectly, Lord, make us forgive perfectly, so that we may really love our enemies for love of you, and pray fervently to you for them, returning no one evil for evil, anxious only to serve everybody in you.

And lead us not into temptation: Hidden or obvious, sudden or unforeseen.

But deliver us from evil: Present, past, or future. Amen.

(Attributed to Saint Francis of Assisi)

What we do and what we are

Lord, you have given your gospel as salt to the earth and light to the world. Pour out the Spirit of your Son upon those of us who live in the midst of the world and its concerns, so that by what we do and what we are we may build up your kingdom; through the same Christ our Lord. Amen.

(Adapted from Pope Paul VI)

* * *

Reflections

Whether you eat or drink, or whatever you do, do everything for the glory of God.

(1 Corinthians 10.31)

If anything is lacking, it is not writing or speaking (for generally there is a surfeit of these anyway), but silence and work.

(John of the Cross)

Giving is the highest expression of potency... Giving is more joyous than receiving, not because it is a deprivation, but because in the act of giving lies the expression of my aliveness.

(Erich Fromm)

The good pleasure of your will

Grant me, Lord, to know what I ought to know, to love what I ought to love, to praise what delights you most, to value what is precious in your sight, to hate what is offensive to you. Do not allow me to judge according to appearances, nor to pass sentence following the judgement of the ignorant, but to discern with true judgement between things visible and spiritual, and, above all things, to seek to know what is the good pleasure of your will.

(Thomas à Kempis)

Justice and peace

Lord, guide national leaders to establish the rule of justice and peace for the whole human family so that all may enjoy that harmony which is a foretaste of your heavenly kingdom. We ask this through Christ our Lord. Amen.

(Anon)

Lord, why are you silent?

Lord, how long shall I call for help and you will not listen? Or cry to you 'Violence!' and you will not save? Why do you make me see wrong-doing and look at trouble? Destruction and violence are before me; strife and contention arise. The wicked surround the righteous – therefore judgement comes forth perverted. Are you not from of old, Lord my God, my Holy One? You shall not die. Your eyes are too pure to behold evil. Lord, why are you silent?

(Adapted from Habakkuk 1.2–4, 12–13)

Make us wholly yours

God of power, make us wholly yours in soul and body, and let our whole life be one of sincere service of you. Increase in us a longing for yourself. Help the prayer that falters on our lips, and, by your power, overcome the enemy within us; through Christ your Son, our Lord. Amen.

(Gothic Breviary)

I adore you

I adore you, my God, and I want to love you with all my heart. I thank you for having created me, made me a Christian, and preserved me this day. I offer you this evening, and all that is in it. May I do your will and act for your greater glory. Keep me from sin and all evil. May your grace be with me always and with all whom I love. Amen.

(Venerable James Alberione, SSP)

Blessing

May our Lady and all the saints pray for us, and the holy guardian angels watch over us and keep us under their protection. And may the blessing of God almighty, the Father, the Son, and the Holy Spirit descend upon us and remain with us always. Amen.

(Adapted from Anthony de Vere)

* * *

Reflections

Do not be overcome by evil, but overcome evil with good.

(Romans 12.21)

Man infinitely surpasses man.

(Blaise Pascal)

Those who pray only when they feel ready for prayer are using prayer to further their self-love.

(Capuchin documents)

The Holy Spirit

Breathe into me, Holy Spirit, that my mind may turn to what
is holy.
Move me, Holy Spirit, that I may do what is holy.
Stir me, Holy Spirit, that I may love what is holy.
Strengthen me, Holy Spirit, that I may preserve what is holy.
Protect me, Holy Spirit, that I may never lose what is holy.

(Saint Augustine)

Willing and ready

Lord, although rich, you became poor for our sakes, and
promised in the gospel that whatever is done to the least of our
brothers and sisters is done to you. Give us grace, we ask you, to
respond to the needs of our fellow-creatures, and to spread the
blessings of your kingdom all over the world, to your praise and
glory, who are God over all, blessed for ever.

(Saint Augustine)

All who suffer illness

Comfort, Lord, all who suffer illness of mind or body. Bring
them healing as you will through the care of doctors and nurses.
Bless the many others who work behind the scenes to support
them. We ask you, Father, to hear this prayer in Jesus' name.
Amen.

(Adapted from the Catholic Truth Society)

God help my thoughts!

God help my thoughts! They stray from me, setting off on the
wildest journeys. When I am in a church, they run off like
naughty children, quarrelling and making trouble. When I read
the Bible, they fly to a distant city. My thoughts can cross an
ocean with a single leap; they can fly from earth to heaven, and
back again, in a single second. They come to me for a fleeting
moment, and then away they go again. No chains, no locks can

hold them back; no threats of punishment can restrain them, no hiss of a lash can frighten them. They slip from my grasp like tails of eels; they swoop hither and thither like swallows in flight. Dear chaste Christ, who can see into every heart and read every mind, take hold of my thoughts. Bring my thoughts back to me, and clasp me to yourself.

(Celtic)

May we be found faithful

God, you work in us unceasingly, and you give each of us our appointed task. Help us steadfastly to fulfil the duties of our calling. When we are called to account, may we be found faithful, and enter into your eternal joy; through the same Jesus Christ our Lord. Amen.

(Adapted from an Anglican source)

* * *

Reflections

The Holy Spirit is God's gift to those who obey him.

(Adapted from Acts 5.32)

If you want to love Christ, spread charity all over the earth, because the members of Christ are all over the world.

(Saint Augustine)

Following Christ is not an outward imitation . . . it means becoming conformed to him.

(Adapted from Pope John Paul II)

Children of your household

You, Father of all, are the beginning of all, the light eternal and the source of all light; you call us in our weakness from the dust and raise us up out of corruption. And so you have called us through your beloved Son to the freedom and dignity of children of your household. Grant us to be saintly children; may we not be unworthy of such a title, but fulfil our calling through the holiness of our lives. May we do so with purity of heart and clean minds; through Christ our Lord. Amen.

(Liturgy of Saint Denis)

Prayer and praise

God of hope, true light of faithful souls and brightness of the blessed, who are truly the light of the world, grant that our hearts may render you a worthy prayer and always glorify you with the offering of praise; through Jesus Christ our Lord. Amen.

(Gelasian Sacramentary)

My path to you

Grant me, I ask you, almighty and most merciful God, that I may fervently desire, wisely search out, and perfectly fulfil all that is well-pleasing to you. Arrange the circumstances of my life to the glory of your name. Grant me knowledge of all that you wish me to do, the desire to do it, and the ability to do it as I ought. May my path to you be safe, straightforward and constant until the end. Give me, Lord, a steadfast heart which no unworthy affection may have power to drag downwards; give me an unconquerable heart which no trouble can wear down, an upright heart which no unworthy motive may draw aside from its purpose. Give me also, Lord my God, understanding to know you, diligence to seek you, and a loyalty that will finally embrace you. Amen.

(Adapted from Saint Thomas Aquinas)

He lives with us

Father, hear our prayers; and as we trust that the Saviour of humankind is seated with you in your majesty, so may we feel that he lives with us to the end of the world, as he has promised; through the same Christ our Lord. Amen.

(Adapted from the Leonine Sacramentary)

Angel of God

Angel of God, appointed by God's mercy to be my guardian, enlighten and protect, direct and govern me this night. Amen.

(Anon)

Blessing

May the God of all patience and consolation grant to all the members of our family that they may live in harmony with one another. With one heart, may we give glory to God our Father, and to Jesus Christ our brother, in the unity and love of the Holy Spirit. Amen.

(Anon)

* * *

Reflections

Prayer of adoration – the essence of true prayer – serves no 'useful purpose', in the strict sense of the term, and, so long as one fails to see this, one can never really know how to pray.

(René Voillaume)

We are foolish to look for 'signs' on the way – it is a form of spiritual materialism that Jesus rebuked – because if we *are* on the way, which means in the Mystery, in the bright cloud of God's presence, then all things are signs. Everything mediates the love of God.

(John Main)

For the ways of the Lord are right, and the upright walk in them.

(Hosea 14.9)

Into your hands, Lord

Into your hands, Lord God, we commend ourselves and all who are dear to us this day. Let the gift of your presence be with us even to its close. Grant that we may never lose sight of you all the day long, but worship you and pray to you, so that in the evening we may again give you thanks; through Christ our Lord. Amen.

(Adapted from the Gelasian Sacramentary)

May your name be praised

God of truth, Father, Son and Holy Spirit, hear our prayer for those who do not know you so that your name may be praised among all peoples of the world. Sustain and inspire your servants who bring them the gospel. Bring fresh vigour to wavering faith; sustain our faith when it is still fragile. Renew our missionary zeal. Make us witnesses to your goodness, full of love, of strength, and of faith, for your glory and for the salvation of the world. Amen.

(Pope Paul VI)

The food of your word

God, you have taught us that we do not live on bread alone, but by every word that comes from the mouth of God; grant us always to hunger for the food of your word, which you have given for our nourishment to eternal life; through Christ our Lord. Amen.

(Adapted from an Anglican source)

Truth is rejoicing in you

Happiness is the possession of the truth, and truth is rejoicing in you, Lord, who are my light, my salvation, my God. This happiness, this life, the only life, is what we seek. We long to possess the truth, and to be possessed by you, Lord, who are the truth. Grant us this for your love's sake. Amen.

(Saint Augustine)

A song of God's children

The law of the Spirit of life in Christ Jesus has set us free from
the law of sin and of death.
All who are led by the Spirit of God are children of God.
When we cry 'Abba! Father!' it is that very Spirit bearing witness
with our spirit that we are children of God; and if children, then
heirs, heirs of God and joint heirs with Christ – if, in fact, we
suffer with him so that we also may be glorified with him.
I consider that the sufferings of this present time are not worth
comparing with the glory about to be revealed to us.
For the creation waits with eager longing for the revealing of
the children of God.

(Adapted from Romans 8.2, 14–19)

Peace of mind

Lord, make us able to walk blamelessly, to act justly, to speak
truthfully, and to give no welcome to speaking badly of our
neighbour. Then we shall know that peace of mind to which
sincerity gives the only true claim.

(Spanish Collect, seventh century)

* * *

Reflections

The people of our day are more impressed by witnesses than by
teachers, and if they listen to these, it is because they also bear
witness.

(Pope Paul VI)

The truth can impose itself on the human mind only in virtue
of its own truth.

(Adapted from Saint Thomas Aquinas)

Jesus said, 'My grace is sufficient for you, for my power is made
perfect in weakness.'

(2 Corinthians 12.8)

Thank you for my friends

Lord, I thank you for my friends, for those who understand me better than I understand myself, for those who know me at my worst and still love me, for those who have forgiven me when I had no right to expect to be forgiven. Help me to be as true to my friends as I would wish them to be true to me. Help me to take the first step to get in touch again with friends from whom I have drifted apart. And help me to have no bitterness, but only forgiveness, to any of my friends who failed or who turned against me; through Jesus Christ our Lord. Amen.

(Adapted from William Barclay)

Grant peace

In your loving-kindness, God, grant peace to all who love you. Since you delight in the nobility of true kindness, renew kindness in us. May the grace of charity free us from all that tears down. Only let the spirit of peace be in our hearts, and we shall overcome all anger, resentment and hostility. This charity shall atone for our many sins. We ask this in Jesus' name. Amen.

(Gothic Breviary)

A sense of humour

Give us a sense of humour, Lord, and also things to laugh about; give us the grace to take a joke against ourselves, and to see the funny side of the things we do; save us from annoyance, bad temper, resentfulness against our friends. Help us to laugh even in the face of trouble, fill our minds with the love of Jesus; for his name's sake.

(Michael Hollings and Etta Gullick)

This household

Heavenly Father, we ask you to give this household, and each member of it, a desire and a hunger for spiritual things, for holiness and for the love of heaven. Grant that whatever is true, whatever is honourable, whatever is just, whatever is pure, whatever is pleasing, whatever is commendable, if there is any excellence and if there is anything worthy of praise, may we think about these things, and, by the help of your Holy Spirit, may we order our lives and our characters according to them; through Jesus Christ our Lord. Amen.

(Adapted from Philippians 4.8)

I believe that you accept me

My God, Jesus revealed you as a waiting Father, full of compassion and love, ever willing to welcome anyone who turns to you. I believe that you accept me just as I am; help me to accept myself. I believe that your arms are open to receive me; help me to cast myself into them. I believe that you hear me even before I begin to pray, and that you know my heart's deepest desires. You are with me here right now, loving me, forgiving me, finding joy in my being with you. And so I can come to you with great confidence, knowing that all you want is my trust.

(Elizabeth Ruth Obbard)

Blessing

The God and Father of the Lord Jesus – blessed be he for ever! – be with us for ever. Amen.

(Adapted from 2 Corinthians 11.31)

* * *

Reflections

The arms race is one of the greatest curses on the human race, and the harm it inflicts on the poor is more than can be endured.

(Vatican II, Gaudium et Spes)

Brothers and sisters, do not be children in your thinking; rather, be infants in evil, but in thinking be adults.

(1 Corinthians 14.20)

If you can't do the best, do the best you can.

(Andrew Carew)

Deliver us from fear

Lord, we ask you to deliver us from fear of the unknown future: from fear of failure; from fear of poverty; from fear of bereavement; from fear of loneliness; from fear of sickness and pain; from fear of age; and from fear of death. Help us, Father, by your grace to love you above all, and to fear nothing. Fill our hearts with cheerful courage and loving trust in you; through our Lord and Master, Jesus Christ. Amen.

(Adapted from Akanu Ibraim, Nigeria)

I trust in you, Lord

I trust in you, Lord, for safety; all the good things I have come from you. You, Lord, are all I have, and you give me all I need; my future is in your hands. I feel completely secure because you protect me from the power of death. You will not abandon me; you will show me the path that leads to life. Your presence fills me with joy and brings me pleasure forever.

(Adapted from Psalm 16)

Freed from our sinful ways

God our Father, when your Son was born of the virgin Mary, he became like us in all things but sin. May we who have been reborn in him be freed from our sinful ways; through Christ our Lord. Amen.

(Adapted from the Roman liturgy)

Perseverance until death

Dear Redeemer, relying on your promises, because you are faithful, all-powerful and merciful, we hope, through the merits of your passion, for the forgiveness of our sins, perseverance until death in your grace, and, at length, by your mercy, to see and love you eternally in heaven. Amen.

(Adapted from Alphonsus Liguori)

A watchful driver

Lord, make me a watchful and careful driver, so that I may not cause pain or death through neglect or carelessness. Protect all who travel with me so that no harm may come to them. Lord Jesus Christ, be with me on my journeys and always bring me home safely and in peace. At the end of life's journey, meet me and welcome me to my true home in heaven with you. Amen.

(Anon)

A spirit of service

Lord of all things in heaven and earth, Lord of the land and the sea and all that is in them, take from us, we ask you, the spirit of greed and covetousness, and give us a spirit of service, so that no one may be in want, but that all, according to their need, may share in your generous goodness; for the love of your only Son Jesus Christ our Lord. Amen.

(Adapted from an Anglican source)

* * *

Reflections

Fear is nothing but a giving up of the helps that come from reason.

(Wisdom 17.12)

When a soul holds on to trust in God – whether in seeking him or contemplating him – this is the highest worship it can bring.

(Julian of Norwich)

Few of us can do great things; all of us can do small things with great love.

(Mother Teresa of Calcutta)

Relatives and friends

God our Father, look kindly on our relatives and friends. By the power of your Holy Spirit, pour out on them the gifts of your love. Give them health of mind and body, that they may love you with all their heart, and do your will in all things; through Christ our Lord. Amen.

(Pope Paul VI)

A new commandment

God of love, through your Son, you have given us a new commandment, that we should love one another as you have loved us, unworthy and wandering as we are. We ask you to give us, your servants, during our stay on earth, a mind forgetful of past ill-will, a pure conscience, and a heart to love others; through your Son Jesus Christ, our Lord. Amen.

(Adapted from the Coptic liturgy)

If I become angry

Father, if I become angry, do not let my anger lead me into sin; do not let me use harmful words, but words that build up and do good to those who hear me; and do not let me make your Holy Spirit sad. Help me to get rid of all bitterness and hate; help me to be kind and tender-hearted, to forgive, as you have forgiven me through Christ our Lord. Amen.

(Adapted from Ephesians 4)

Free me from all evils

Chosen Leader and Lord, conqueror of hell, I, your creature and servant, delivered from eternal death, magnify and praise you who are infinitely merciful; free me from all evils as I call upon you: Jesus, Son of God, have mercy upon me. Amen.

(Orthodox)

Sorrow for sin

My God, I am heartily sorry for having offended you, and I detest all my sins, because they have offended you, my God, who are all good and deserving of my love. I firmly resolve, with the help of your grace, to do my best to sin no more and to avoid the occasions of sin. Amen.

(Anon)

Blessing

May the right hand of the Lord keep us in our old age;
may the grace of Christ defend us from the enemy;
and may the Lord direct our hearts in the way of peace. Amen.

(Adapted from the Book of Cerne)

* * *

Reflections

Cheap grace is the deadly enemy of our church. We are fighting
today for costly grace. Cheap grace means grace sold on the mar-
ket like huckster's wares. The sacraments, the forgiveness of sin
and the consolations of religion are thrown away at cut prices.
Cheap grace is the preaching of forgiveness without requiring
repentance, baptism without church discipline, communion
without confession, absolution without personal confession.
Cheap grace is grace without discipleship, grace without the
cross, grace without Jesus Christ, living and incarnate.

Costly grace is the treasure hidden in the field; for the sake of
it people will gladly go and sell all that they have. It is the pearl of
great price to buy which the merchant will sell all his goods. It is
the kingly rule of Christ, for whose sake people will pluck out the
eyes which cause them to stumble; it is the call of Jesus Christ at
which disciples leave their nets and follow him.

Such grace is *costly* because it calls us to follow, and it is *grace*
because it calls us to follow *Jesus Christ*. It is costly because it
costs people their lives, and it is grace because it gives a person
the only true life.

(Adapted from Dietrich Bonhoeffer)

The effect of righteousness will be peace, and the result of righteousness, quietness and trust forever.

(Isaiah 32.17)

My Lord and my God, how great are your wonders! We are here
below like simple shepherds; and yet we understand something
of you. But truly it can be hardly more than nothing, because we
ourselves are a mystery.

(Teresa of Avila)

I have put my trust in you

Make your mercy known to me in this morning hour, Lord, for I have put my trust in you. I have now lifted up my heart to you, so show me, Lord, the way I must walk. Amen.

(Adapted from the Gothic Breviary)

Christ's Cross

Christ's cross over this face, and thus over my ear. Christ's cross over this eye.

Christ's cross over this nose.

Christ's cross before me to accompany me. Christ's cross behind me to accompany me.

Christ's cross to meet every difficulty both in hollow and on hill.

Christ's cross eastward facing me. Christ's cross back towards the sunset. In the north, in the south, increasingly may Christ's cross straightaway be.

Christ's cross up to broad heaven. Christ's cross down to earth. Let no evil or hurt come to my body or soul.

Christ's cross over me as I sit. Christ's cross over me as I lie. Christ's cross be all my strength until we reach the Kingdom of heaven.

From the top of my head to the nail of my foot, Lord, Christ, against every danger I trust in the protection of the cross.

Till the day of my death, going into the clay – Christ's cross over this face.

(Adapted from the Celtic)

God the source of life

God, with whom there is the source of life and by whose light we are lightened, foster in us the nobility of knowledge so that at this life-giving spring we may quench our thirst. Bring to our darkened minds the heavenly light of intelligence; in Jesus' name. Amen.

(Adapted from the Gothic Breviary)

Serve you faithfully

Grant us, Lord, a true knowledge of salvation, so that, freed from fear and from the power of our foes, we may serve you faithfully all the days of our life. We make this prayer through Christ our Lord. Amen.

(Adapted from the Roman liturgy)

For one who has died

God, you have called (*name*) from this life. Father of all mercy, fulfil her (his) faith in you, and lead her (him) safely home to heaven, to be happy with you for ever. Amen.

(Adapted from the Roman liturgy)

* * *

Reflections

When Christ commends his spirit into the hands of his Father, he commends himself to God as man in order to commend all people to God.

(Saint Athanasius)

When the goodness and loving kindness of God our Saviour appeared, he saved us, not because of any works of righteousness that we had done, but according to his mercy, through the water of rebirth and renewal by the Holy Spirit.

(Titus 3.4–5)

God created us without us, but he did not will to save us without us.

(Saint Augustine)

23

Passion of Jesus

Good and gentle Jesus, I kneel before you. I see and ponder your five wounds. My eyes see what David prophesied about you, 'They have pierced my hands and my feet; they have counted all my bones.' Engrave on me this image of yourself. Fulfil the yearnings of my heart: give me faith, hope and love, repentance for my sins and true conversion of life. Amen.

(Adapted from the Roman liturgy)

Protect me this night

My God, I adore you and I wish to love you with all my heart. I thank you for having created me and saved me by your grace, and for having preserved me during this day. I pray that you will take for yourself whatever good I may have done this day, and that you will forgive me whatever evil I have done. Protect me this night, and may your grace always be with me and with those I love. Amen.

(Adapted from Pope Paul VI)

Enlighten that darkness

Lord, you have lighted in my soul a light by which I see, and truly I am often frightened at my own darkness. Enlighten that darkness which is within me so that I may feel my emotions to be under control; so that I may appreciate, and rightly and justly seek, what is worthy of your love.

(Adapted from Saint Bernard of Clairvaux)

Help me to forgive

God and Father of us all, you have forgiven my sins and sent me your peace. Help me to forgive my neighbour and to work with the people I meet to establish peace and unity in this world. Amen.

(Anon)

One more miracle

Son of God, perform a miracle for me: change my heart. You whose crimson blood redeems humankind, purify my heart. It is you who makes the sun bright and the ice sparkle; you who makes the rivers flow and the salmon leap. Your skilled hand makes the nut tree blossom, and the wheat turn golden; your spirit composes the songs of the birds and the buzz of the bees. Your creation is a million wondrous miracles, beautiful to behold. I ask of you just one more miracle: beautify my soul.

(Celtic)

Blessing

May God make us steadfast in faith, joyful in hope, and untiring in love all the days of our life.

(Adapted from the Roman liturgy)

* * *

Reflections

If you forgive others their trespasses, your heavenly Father will also forgive you; but if you do not forgive others, neither will your Father forgive your trespasses.

(Matthew 6.14–15)

We have laboured so long under the delusion that corrections, criticism, and punishments stimulate a person to grow. We have rationalized the taking out of our unhappiness and incompleteness in many destructive ways.

(John Powell)

Little satisfies necessity; nothing satisfies sensuality.

(Capuchin documents)

The Angelus

The angel of the Lord declared unto Mary;
and she conceived of the Holy Spirit.

Hail Mary, full of grace, the Lord is with you. Blessed are you
among women, and blessed is the fruit of your womb,
Jesus. Holy Mary, Mother of God, pray for us sinners now,
and at the hour of our death. Amen.

Behold the handmaid of the Lord;
be it done unto me according to your word.

Hail Mary (*as above*)

And the Word was made flesh;
and dwelt amongst us.

Hail Mary (*as above*)

Pray for us, holy Mother of God:
that we may be made worthy of the promises of Christ.

Let us pray:

Pour forth, we beseech you, Lord, your grace into our hearts,
that we, to whom the incarnation of Christ your Son was
made known by the message of an angel, may be brought
by his passion and cross to the glory of his resurrection;
through the same Christ our Lord. Amen.

(Adapted from Luke 1.26–38)

This day in gladness and peace

Let my prayer, Lord, come before you this morning. You took to
yourself our weak and tempted nature. Grant me to pass this day
in gladness and peace, so that, reaching the evening without
stumbling or falling, I may praise you, the everlasting King, who
lives and rules, world without end. Amen.

(Mozarabic liturgy)

Bless our children

We pray to you, almighty and kindly Father, creator of this
world and giver of life. Though awe-inspiring, you are gentle

and merciful, and deserving of all praise. Lord Jesus, you who laid your hand of blessing on children, we ask you to bless our children. Give them wisdom and increase of goodness. Let them find joy in you, love you and value you. May they reverence you and keep your commandments. So, by your grace, God and Saviour of the world, may they come to the full length of days. Amen.

(Adapted from the Roman liturgy, fifteenth century)

* * *

Reflections

The best is sometimes the enemy of the good.

(Anon)

Love children especially, for, like the angels, they too are sinless, and they live to soften and purify our hearts, and, as it were, to guide us. Woe to them who offend a child!

(Fyodor Dostoevsky)

Better is a dry morsel with quiet than a house full of feasting with strife.

(Proverbs 17.1)

An instrument of your peace

Lord, make me an instrument of your peace:
where there is hatred, let me sow love;
where there is discord, harmony;
where there is injury, pardon;
where there is error, truth;
where there is doubt, faith;
where there is despair, hope;
where there is darkness, light;
where there is sadness, joy.

Divine Master,
grant that I may not so much seek:
to be consoled, as to console;
to be understood, as to understand;
to be loved, as to love.
For it is in giving that we receive;
it is in forgetting self that we find ourselves;
it is in pardoning that we are pardoned;
and it is in dying that we are born to eternal life.

(Attributed to Saint Francis of Assisi)

Avoid unchastity

Help me, God, to avoid unchastity; to remember that my body
is the temple of your Holy Spirit who lives within me; that I do
not belong to myself but to you, and for your glory.

(Adapted from 1 Corinthians 6.18–20)

I have sinned against you

Father of mercy, like the prodigal in the parable I return to you
and say: 'I have sinned against you and am no longer worthy to
be called your child.' Christ Jesus, saviour of the world, I pray
with the repentant thief to whom you promised paradise: 'Lord,
remember me in your kingdom.' Holy Spirit, fountain of love, I

call on you with trust: 'Purify my heart and help me to walk as a child of light.'

(Adapted from the Roman liturgy)

Bless and guard our family

May the God of peace bless and guard our family. May we follow his will in all that we do, and may we be ever more pleasing to him. Amen.

(Pope Paul VI)

* * *

Reflections

Do you not know that you are God's temple and that God's Spirit dwells in you? If anyone destroys God's temple, God will destroy that person. For God's temple is holy, and you are that temple.

(1 Corinthians 3.16–17)

At the Last Supper, on the night he was betrayed, our Saviour instituted the eucharistic sacrifice of his body and blood. This he did in order to perpetuate the sacrifice of the cross throughout the ages until he should come again, and so to entrust to his beloved spouse, the church, a memorial of his death and resurrection: a sacrament of love, a sign of unity, a bond of charity, a paschal banquet in which Christ is consumed, the mind is filled with grace, and a pledge of future glory is given to us.

(Vatican II, Sacrosanctum Concilium, based on Saint Thomas Aquinas)

Let your marriage sustain your love.

(Dietrich Bonhoeffer to a newly married couple)

King of blest Sunday

A hundred thousand welcomes to you, king of blest Sunday, who has come to help us after the week. Guide my feet early to the Eucharist, open my lips with blest words, stir up my heart and banish out of it all spite. I look up to the Son of Mary, her one and only Son of mercy, for he it is who has so excellently redeemed us, and his we are whether we live or die. A hundred thousand welcomes to you, king of glorious Sunday. Son of the virgin and king of glory, sweet Jesus, son of Mary, have mercy on us.

(Celtic)

The Benedictus

Blessed be the Lord God of Israel,
for he has looked favourably on his people and redeemed
 them.
He has raised up a mighty saviour for us in the house of
 his servant David,
as he spoke through the mouth of his holy prophets
 from of old,
that we would be saved from our enemies and from the
 hands of all who hate us.
Thus he has shown the mercy promised to our ancestors,
and has remembered his holy covenant,
the oath that he swore to our ancestor Abraham, to grant
 us that we,
being rescued from the hands of our enemies,
might serve him without fear,
in holiness and righteousness before him all our days.
And you, child, will be called the prophet of the Most High;
for you will go before the Lord to prepare his ways,
to give knowledge of salvation to his people
by the forgiveness of their sins.
By the tender mercy of our God,

the dawn from on high will break upon us,
to give light to those who sit in darkness and in the
    shadow of death,
to guide our feet into the way of peace.

(Luke 1.68–79)

The splendour of the resurrection

Let the splendour of the resurrection light up our minds and
hearts, Lord, scattering the shadows of death, and bringing us
to the radiance of eternity; through Christ our Lord. Amen.

(Adapted from the Roman liturgy)

The companionship of eternal redemption

Lord, only king and wondrous beyond all telling, be always ready
to help those who praise and glorify your name, that they may
make progress in true devotion, be always under your loving
care, and, with you as leader, come at last to the companionship
of eternal redemption; in Jesus' name. Amen.

(Pontifical of Magdalen)

* * *

Reflections

The sabbath was made for humankind, not humankind for the
sabbath.

(Mark 2.27)

The liturgy is an incomparable school of spirituality.

(Pope Paul VI)

How can we learn to stop talking and to start listening? From
'strenuous' to 'self-acting' prayer . . . from 'my' prayer to the
prayer of *Christ in me*?

(Kallistos Ware)

The resurrection of Christ

We have seen the resurrection of Christ; let us worship the holy Lord Jesus, who alone is without sin. We venerate your cross, Lord Christ, and we praise and glorify your holy resurrection. For you are our God, we know no other; upon your name we call. Come, all you faithful, let us venerate the holy resurrection of Christ: since through the cross joy has come to all the world. Always blessing the Lord, we sing the praises of his resurrection: for he endured the cross on our behalf, and has destroyed death by death.

(Orthodox)

Into your hands, Lord

Into your hands, Lord, I commend my soul and my body, my mind and my thoughts, my prayers and my promises, my intentions and my attempts, my going out and my coming in, my words and my works, my senses and my limbs, my life and my death.

(Adapted from Gilbert Shaw)

The perfect unity of your love

Father, Son and Holy Spirit, holy and undivided Trinity, three Persons in one God: inspire your people gathered in your name to witness to the perfect unity of your love, one God, now and for ever. Amen.

(Adapted from the Society of Saint Francis)

Prayer in time of distress

Lord, do not reprove me in your anger; punish me not
   in your rage.
Have mercy on me, Lord, I have no strength.
Lord, heal me, my body is racked; my soul is racked with pain.
But you, Lord . . . how long? Return, Lord, rescue my soul.
Save me in your merciful love. I am exhausted with
   my groaning;

Every night I drench my pillow with tears; I bedew
    my bed with weeping.
My eye wastes away with grief; I have grown old
    surrounded by my foes.
Leave me, all you who do evil; for the Lord has heard
    my weeping.
The Lord has accepted my plea; the Lord will accept
    my prayer.

(Adapted from Psalm 6)

Blessing

May the God of steadfastness and encouragement grant us to
live in harmony with one another, in accordance with Christ
Jesus, so that together we may with one voice glorify the God
and Father of our Lord Jesus Christ. Amen.

(Adapted from Romans 15.5–6)

* * *

Reflections

The Lord is in his holy temple; let all the earth keep silence
before him!

(Habakkuk 2.20)

From the hand of God receive everything;
within the hand of God place everything;
into the hand of God entrust everything.

(Anon)

What then is it that we who profess religion lack? This: a willingness to *be* changed, a willingness to allow Almighty God to
change us. We do not like to let go our old selves . . . But when a
person comes to God to be saved, then the essence of true conversion is a *surrender* of oneself, an unreserved unconditional
surrender.

(Adapted from John Henry Newman)

33

You are not far

Almighty God, you have made the world and everything in it. You are Lord of heaven and earth. You give life and breath to everyone. We look for you, yet indeed you are not far from each one of us. For in you we live and move and have our being.

(Adapted from Acts 17.27–28)

I offer you this new day

Jesus Lord, I offer you this new day because I believe in you, love you, hope all things in you, and thank you for your blessings. I am sorry for having offended you and forgive everyone who has offended me. Lord, look on me and leave in me peace and courage and your humble wisdom that I may serve others with joy, and be pleasing to you all day.

(Anon)

When I fail

My God, when I fail, especially in something I so much wanted to do well, don't let me try to put the blame on everyone and everything except myself. Don't let me be resentful and bitter about it, but help me to accept both success and failure with a good grace. Don't let me be envious and jealous of those who have succeeded where I have failed. Don't ever let me talk about giving up and giving in; but help me to refuse to be beaten. Help me to learn the lesson which you want me to learn even from failure; help me to begin again, and not to make the same mistakes again. Maybe it is hardest of all to meet the eyes of those who are disappointed in me. Help me even yet to show them that I deserve their trust and to let them see what I can do. This I ask for your love's sake. Amen.

(Adapted from William Barclay)

I thank you

He who made me is good, and he is my own good. I rejoice in his goodness which, even in childhood, filled my existence. I thank you in whom I place my confidence and my trust. I thank you, loving God, for all your gifts, and ask you to keep them for me.

(Adapted from Saint Augustine)

United in peace and love

Sovereign and almighty Lord, bless all your people. Give us your peace, your help, your love that we may be united in peace and love, one body and one spirit, in one hope of our calling, in your divine and boundless love; for the sake of Jesus Christ, the great shepherd of your people. Amen.

(Adapted from the liturgy of Saint Mark)

* * *

Reflections

Once God is forgotten, the creature is lost sight of as well.

(Vatican II, Gaudium et Spes)

God, give me grace to be faithful in action, and indifferent as to the success.

(François de la Mothe Fénélon)

Christianity is not for losers but for those who are not afraid to be losers ... The Christian faith is for those who forgive because they are not afraid of losing.

(Gerald O'Collins)

Out of the depths

Out of the depths I cry to you, Lord.
Lord, hear my voice!
Let your ears be attentive to the voice of my pleading!
If you, Lord, should mark our guilt, Lord, who would
      survive?
But with you is found forgiveness: for this we revere you.
My soul is waiting for the Lord, I count on his word.
My soul is longing for the Lord more than the watchman
      for daybreak.
Because with the Lord there is mercy and fullness of
      redemption.
Israel indeed he will redeem from all its iniquity.

(Adapted from Psalm 130)

Putting God first

Lord God, I know that if I do not love you with all my heart,
with all my mind, with all my soul and with all my strength, I
shall love something else with all my heart and mind and soul
and strength. Grant that, putting you first in all my loving, I
may be liberated from all lesser loves and loyalties, and have you
as my first love, my chief good and my final joy.

(Adapted from George Appleton)

We bless you for the generous fruits of the earth

Almighty God and heavenly Father, we glorify you that you
have again fulfilled your gracious promise to us, that as long as
the earth lasts, planting-time and harvest shall not fail. We bless
you for the generous fruits of the earth which you have given
for our use. Teach us, we ask you, to remember that it is not by
bread alone that we live. Grant us always to feed on him who is
the true bread from heaven, Jesus Christ our Lord, to whom
with you, and the Holy Spirit, be all honour and glory, for ever
and ever. Amen.

(Adapted from an Anglican source)

I go to sleep with your blessing

I go to sleep with your blessing. One day my last evening will come when I will enter eternity. Let me now so live that all that I do in time may be a preparation for that last blessed peace, so that vision may follow faith, possession succeed hope, perfect union replace imperfect love, for you are my final end and greatest good. Amen.

(Saint Francis de Sales)

Blessing

May the God of peace sanctify us entirely; and may our spirit and soul and body be kept sound and blameless at the coming of our Lord Jesus Christ. The one who calls us is faithful, and he will do this. Amen.

(Adapted from 1 Thessalonians 5.23)

* * *

Reflections

You will never attain to a life of authentic prayer so long as you are looking for an emotional experience. On your part, the value of your prayer depends on the effort it demands of you. On God's part, the value of your prayer depends on the action of the Holy Spirit within you.

(Adapted from Michel Quoist)

So many choose to be lonely in the crowd rather than find communion in solitude. When we are isolated we cannot see beyond ourselves: this is the terrible delusion of self-centredness.

(Adapted from John Main)

My God and my all.

(Saint Thomas Aquinas)

Grace to fix my mind on you

Jesus, grant me grace to fix my mind on you, especially in times of prayer, when I converse directly with you. Stop the motions of my wandering head, and the desires of my unstable heart; suppress the power of my spiritual enemies, who endeavour at that time to draw my mind from heavenly thoughts, to many vain imaginations. So shall I, with joy and gratitude, look on you as my deliverer from all the evils I have escaped; and as my benefactor for all the good I have ever received, or can hope for. I shall see that you are my only good, and that all other things are but means ordained by you to make me fix my mind on you, to make me love you more and more, and, by loving you, to be eternally happy. Beloved of my soul, take all my thoughts here, so that my eyes, abstaining from vain and hurtful sights, may become worthy to behold you face to face in your glory for ever. Amen.

(Richard Whitford)

Love and loving-kindness

Where love and loving-kindness are together, God is in their midst. Christ's love has gathered us together in one company. Rejoice then, and delight in him.
Revere and love the living God. Let us love one another without reserve or deception.
Where love and loving-kindness are together, God is in their midst. Therefore, when we are gathered together in one company, we must not be divided from one another in our feelings. Spite, quarrelling and strife must not be found among us.
May Christ, who is God, be in our midst.
Where love and loving-kindness are together, God is in their midst. May it be ours, gathered together in the company of the saints, to see you, Christ our Lord, in your glory. May this happiness of immeasurable excellence be ours through unending ages. Amen.

(Adapted from the Roman liturgy)

I give thanks to God

I give thanks tirelessly to God who kept me faithful in the day of trial, so that today I offer sacrifice to him confidently, the living sacrifice of my life to Christ, my Lord, who preserved me in all my troubles. I can say, therefore: Who am I, Lord, and what is my calling that you should cooperate with me? I praise and proclaim your name in all places, not only when things go well but also in times of stress. Whether I receive good or ill, I return thanks equally to God, who taught me always to trust him unreservedly.

(Attributed to Saint Patrick)

Send your Spirit

God of our Lord Jesus Christ, Father of glory, send your Spirit to make us wise and reveal you to us, so that we know you. Open our minds to see your light so that we may know what is the hope to which you have called us, how rich the blessings you promise us, how great is the power at work in us who believe. We ask this in Jesus' name. Amen.

(Adapted from Ephesians 1.17–19)

* * *

Reflections

It is far easier for me to lift my soul to God than my hand to my head.

(Jan van Ruysbroeck)

Love is the fulfilling of the law.

(Romans 13.10)

Without the Holy Spirit, God is far away, Christ stays in the past, the gospel is a dead letter, the church is simply an organization, authority a matter of domination, mission a matter of propaganda, the liturgy no more than an evocation, Christian living a slave morality. But, in the Holy Spirit, the cosmos is resurrected and groans with the birth-pangs of the kingdom, the risen Christ is there, the gospel is the power of life, the church shows forth the life of the Trinity, authority is a liberating service, mission is a Pentecost, the liturgy is both memorial and realization, human action is deified.

(Adapted from Ignatios of Latakia)

By your grace

By your grace, God, we do not suffer total death. You warn us
to be watchful. By your grace we distinguish good from evil, we
can shun evil and seek good and not fall into adversity. By your
grace we are enabled both to command and to obey. By your
grace we discover that sometimes what we think is ours is alien
to us and what we think is alien is ours. By your grace we are
freed from the snares and attacks of evil. It is through you that
little things do not make us small. By your grace the best in us
is not suffocated by the worst in us. By your grace death is
swallowed up in victory. God, you lead us to yourself and strip
us of what exists no more in order to clothe us in what does
exist. God, you make us worthy to be heard by you. You
strengthen us and make us know all truth. You offer us that
good which stops us from becoming fools, and you do not
allow others to make us foolish. You lead us back onto the right
path. You take us right up to the door and open it wide to those
who knock. You give us the bread of life and, by your grace,
we drink of the water which takes away all thirst. You convict
the world of sin, of justice, and of judgement. By your grace we
are not troubled by those who do not believe. By your grace
we are not slaves to weakness and disease. God who purifies us
and prepares us for divine rewards, come to me in your favour.
Amen.

(Adapted from Saint Augustine)

Your word is a lamp for my steps

Your word is a lamp for my steps and a light for my path.
I have sworn and have made up my mind to obey your
    decrees.
Lord, I am deeply afflicted: by your word give me life.
Accept, Lord, the homage of my lips and teach me your
    decrees.

Though I carry my life in my hands, I remember your law.
Though the wicked try to ensnare me I do not stray from
  your precepts.
Your will is my heritage for ever, the joy of my heart.
I set myself to carry out your will in fullness, for ever.

(Adapted from Psalm 119)

Blessing

May grace and peace be ours in abundance in the knowledge of
God and of Jesus our Lord. Amen.

(Adapted from 1 Peter 1.2)

* * *

Reflections

There, but for the grace of God, go I.

*(Attributed to Saint Francis of Assisi on seeing someone
spoken of as a sinner)*

Love's finest speech is without words.

(Hadewijch of Brabant)

When you make a promise to God, do not delay fulfilling it; for
he has no pleasure in fools. Fulfil what you promise.

(Ecclesiastes 5.4)

Grant us your help

Lord, from whom to be turned is to fall, to whom to be turned is to rise, in whom to stand is to live for ever; grant us in all our duties your help, in all our problems your guidance, in all our dangers your protection, in all our sorrows your peace; through Jesus Christ our Lord. Amen.

(Adapted from Saint Augustine)

You do not fall

As the rain hides the stars, as the autumn mist hides the hills, as the clouds veil the blue of the sky, so the dark happenings of my life hide the shining of your face from me. Yet if I may hold your hand in the darkness, it is enough. Since I know that although I may stumble in my going, you do not fall.

(Celtic)

Give us your unreserved willingness for service

Most blessed virgin Mary, mother of Christ and mother of the church, with joy and wonder we seek to make our own your *Magnificat*, joining you in your hymn of thankfulness and love.

With you we give thanks to God 'whose mercy is from generation to generation', for the exalted vocation and the many forms of mission entrusted to us. God has called each of us by name to live our own communion of love and holiness, and to be one in the great family of God's children. He has sent us forth to shine with the light of Christ and to communicate the fire of the Spirit in every part of society through a life inspired by the gospel.

Virgin of the *Magnificat*, fill our hearts with a gratitude and enthusiasm for this vocation and mission.

With humility and magnanimity you were the 'handmaid of the Lord'; give us your unreserved willingness for service to God and the salvation of the world. Open our hearts to the great anticipation of the kingdom of God and of the proclamation of the gospel to the whole of creation. Your mother's heart is ever mindful of the many dangers and evils which threaten to over-power the men and women of our time. At the same time your heart also takes notice of the many initiatives undertaken for good, the great yearning for values, and the progress achieved in bringing forth the abundant fruits of salvation.

Virgin full of courage, may your spiritual strength and trust in God inspire us, so that we might know how to overcome all the obstacles that we encounter in accomplishing our mission. Teach us to treat the affairs of the world with a real sense of Christian responsibility and a joyful hope of the coming of God's kingdom, and of a 'new heavens and a new earth'.

You who were gathered in prayer with the apostles in the cenacle, awaiting the coming of the Spirit at Pentecost, implore his renewed outpouring on all us faithful, men and women alike, so that we might more fully respond to our vocation and mission, as branches engrafted to the true vine, called to bear much fruit for the life of the world. Virgin Mother, guide and sustain us so that we might always live as true sons and daughters of the church of your Son. Enable us to do our part in helping to establish on earth the civilization of truth and love, as God wills it, for his glory. Amen.

(Pope John Paul II)

* * *

Reflections

Be careful, then, how you live, not as unwise people but as wise, making the most of time.

(Adapted from Ephesians 5.15–16)

We are servants of God by nature; we are children of God by grace.

(Anon)

Every act which is performed so that we may be united with God in holy companionship is a true sacrifice.

(Saint Augustine)

God the protector

I lift up my eyes to the mountains: from where shall come
my help?
My help shall come from the Lord who made heaven and
earth.
May he never allow you to stumble! Let him sleep not,
your guard!
No, he sleeps not, nor slumbers, Israel's guard!
The Lord is your guard and your shade; at your right side
he stands.
By day the sun shall not smite you nor the moon in
the night.
The Lord will guard you from evil, he will guard your
soul.
The Lord will guard your going and coming both now
and for ever.

(Adapted from Psalm 121)

Those who wander in doubt

Have mercy, heavenly Father, on those who wander in doubt
and uncertainty amid the darkness of this world, and on all
who are hardened through sin. Grant them grace to come to
themselves, the will and power to return to you, and the loving
welcome of your forgiveness; through Jesus Christ our Lord.
Amen.

(Adapted from an Anglican source)

That I may clearly see

All-wise and all-seeing God, you look upon all my actions, and
see all that I do. Enlighten my understanding that I may clearly
see what sins I have committed, and what good I have left
undone. Move my heart that I may sincerely repent and amend.

(Spend a few moments in silent reflection)

(Anon, India)

I am sorry for all my sins

God our Father, I thank you for loving me. I am sorry for all my sins, for what I have done and for what I have failed to do. I will sincerely try to love you and others in everything I do and say. Help me to walk in your light today and always.

(Adapted from the Roman liturgy)

Give our bodies restful sleep

Lord, give our bodies restful sleep, and let the work we have done today be sown for an eternal harvest; through Christ our Lord. Amen.

(Adapted from the Roman liturgy)

Blessing

The God of love and peace be with us. Amen.

(Adapted from 2 Corinthians 13)

* * *

Reflections

Keep your mind in front of the mirror of eternity! Keep your soul in the radiance of glory! Keep your heart in the image of the divine reality! Change yourself into the image of God through contemplation that you may sense what his friends sense as they taste the secret bliss which God has prepared from the foundation of the world for those who love him.

(Clare of Assisi)

If we cannot be condemned by our own conscience, we need not be ashamed in God's presence.

(1 John 3.21)

Acquire inner peace and thousands around you will find their salvation.

(Seraphim of Sarov)

Help us during this day

God, great and wonderful, you have given us the hope of your promised kingdom through the gifts you have already given us. Help us to avoid all evil during this day, so that, at its close, we may stand without blame before your holy glory and praise you, the God of our life, the lover of humanity; through Christ our Lord. Amen.

(Orthodox)

The mystery of your body and blood

Lord Jesus Christ, you gave to your church an admirable sacrament as the abiding memorial of your passion. Teach us so to worship the sacred mystery of your body and blood, that its redeeming power may sanctify us always, you who live and reign with the Father and the Holy Spirit, God, for ever and ever. Amen.

(Adapted from the Roman liturgy)

For the people of God

Lord our God, your commandments are a light to the earth; teach us to live in holiness and justice since we glorify you, the true God. Hear us, listen to us: remember, Lord, each one of those who pray with us here, and in your power grant them salvation. Make your people grow in holiness, and bless your inheritance; give peace to your world and all your churches, to those who serve you as priests and to our rulers and all your people.

For your Name is worthy of all honour and majesty, and we glorify you in hymns of praise, Father, Son, and Holy Spirit, now and for ever, to the ages of ages. Amen.

(Orthodox)

Remove divisions among Christians

Lord, pour out upon us the fullness of your mercy, and, by the power of your Spirit, remove divisions among Christians. Let your church rise more clearly as a sign for all the nations so that the world may be filled with the light of your Spirit and believe in Jesus Christ whom you have sent, he who lives and reigns with you and the Holy Spirit, one God, for ever and ever. Amen.

(Adapted from the Roman liturgy)

Resting in God

Lord, my heart is not proud nor haughty my eyes.
I have not gone after things too great, nor marvels beyond me.
Truly I have set my soul in silence and peace.
A weaned child on its mother's breast, even so is my soul.
Hope in the Lord, both now and for ever.

(Adapted from Psalm 131)

* * *

Reflections

He cannot have God for his father who has not the church for his mother.

(Saint Cyprian of Carthage)

The Son of Man came not to be served but to serve and to give his life as a ransom for many.

(Mark 10.45)

The church becomes as it were the fullness and completion of the Redeemer, Christ in the church being in some sense brought to complete achievement.

(Saint Thomas Aquinas)

Honour and praise

Honour and praise to you, Lord our God, for all your tender mercies again bestowed on us during this week. Constant thanks be to you for creating us in your own likeness; for redeeming us by the precious blood of your Son when we were lost; and for sanctifying us with the Holy Spirit.

For your help in our necessities, your protection in many dangers of body and soul; your comfort in our sorrows, and for sparing us in life, and giving us enough time to repent; for all the benefits, most merciful Father, that we have received of your goodness, we thank you. And we ask you to grant us always your Holy Spirit, that we may grow in grace, in steadfast faith, and perseverance in all good works; through Jesus Christ our Lord. Amen.

(John Knox)

Open the paths to faith

Open to us your servants, Lord God, all the paths of faith, so that we may reach the safety and strength of the truth. Make it known more fully to us so that we may learn how to avoid error. May we recognize the things that lead to salvation. May we lay aside all that remains within us of untruth. May we receive the brightness of the full light of Christ. May the stain of sin leave us completely. Christ Jesus, you who open all doors and make known the way of salvation, be pleased to love us your servants who have come to the knowledge of your name and your love. May we desire to follow you in our thoughts, you whom we profess with our lips. Amen.

(Anon)

The beauty and meaning of all I see

Lord God, who has given me the gift of sight, grant that I may see not only with the eyes of my head but also with the eyes of my heart, so that I may perceive the beauty and meaning of all

I see, and glorify you, the Creator of all, who are blessed for evermore. Amen.

(Adapted from George Appleton)

You are my hope

Lord God, you are life, wisdom, truth, bounty and blessedness, the Eternal, the one true good. My God and my Lord, you are my hope and my heart's joy. I confess with thanksgiving that you have made me in your image that I may direct all my thoughts to you and love you rightly, that I may more and more love and possess you. And since in the life here below, I cannot fully attain this blessedness, let it at least grow in me day by day, until at last it be fulfilled in the life to come. Here may the knowledge of you be increased, and there may it be perfected. Here may my love of you grow, and there may it ripen, so that my joy being here great in hope may there in fruition be made perfect. Amen.

(Saint Anselm of Canterbury)

Blessing

The grace of the Lord Jesus be with us. Amen.

(Adapted from 1 Corinthians 16.23)

* * *

Reflections

I believe, Lord; help my unbelief.

(Mark 9.24)

Mere inherited faith, in those who can have an intelligent faith, is dangerous and inconsistent.

(John Henry Newman)

We lament that God is powerless over evil, but if he always seemed powerful in our universe, what would be left for us to do? We cannot in the one breath call for freedom, as mankind has always done, and in the next call for continuous divine intervention.

(Seán Ó Conaill)

I welcome this new day

God of my life, I welcome this new day. It is your gift to me, a new creation, a promise of resurrection. I thank you for the grace of being alive this morning. I thank you for the sleep that has refreshed me. I thank you for this chance to make a new beginning. This day, Lord, is full of promise and opportunity; let me waste none of it. This day is full of mystery and the unknown: help me to face it without fear or anxiety. This day is blessed with beauty and adventure: make me fully alive to it.

During this day keep me thoughtful, prayerful and kind. May I be courteous and helpful to others, and not turned in on myself. Keep me from any word or deed that would hurt, or destroy, or belittle. And may the thoughts of my mind be pleasing in your sight.

When night comes again, may I look back on this day with no grievance or bitterness in my heart. And may nobody be unhappy because of anything I have done, or anything I have failed to do. Lord, bless this day for me and everyone. Make it a day in which we grow to have the mind of Christ, your Son. Amen.

(Congregation of the Most Holy Redeemer)

The dignity of service

God our Father, who through the life of your Son has shown us the dignity of service, help us to be courteous and considerate to those who serve us in shops and offices, on our journeys and at work, so that all labour may be held in honour, and people be united in mutual respect; through Christ our Lord. Amen.

(Adapted from an Anglican source)

For those who suffer persecution

Be merciful, Lord, to all our brothers and sisters who suffer any kind of persecution or affliction, whether in mind or body, especially those who suffer for your name and gospel; give them patience, constancy and steadfast hope until you send them full and good deliverance of all their troubles; through Jesus Christ our Lord. Amen.

(Adapted from Christian Prayers, 1566)

The wrong kind of anger

Lord, I discern in my anger a sense of self-righteousness which is much too close to pleasure. And I think of you, Lord. You were never angry in your own defence, and you took no pleasure in anger: else why the cross? But you were angry for God: you were angry with those who sold him as a commodity; you were angry with those who used him for their own status; or who treated him as belonging only to them. Lord, implant in me a fear of the wrong kind of anger, one which panders to my self-importance, or is simply indulging my frustration. Forgive me, Lord, for all such occasions.

(Adapted from Ruth Etchells)

You were led to the cross

Lord Jesus Christ, you were led to the cross to suffer the penalty of death for the salvation of humanity. In your mercy grant us pardon for our past offences, and, by your power, preserve us from future falls; who live and reign for ever and ever. Amen.

(Adapted from the Roman liturgy)

* * *

Reflections

Fight the good fight of the faith; take hold of the eternal life to which you were called.

(1 Timothy 6.12)

Suffering . . . contains within itself a singular challenge to communion and solidarity.

(Pope John Paul II, Salvifici Doloris)

So far as I am concerned, to die in Jesus Christ is better than to be monarch of earth's widest bounds. He who died for us is all that I seek; he who rose again for us is my whole desire. The pangs of birth are upon me; have patience with me, and do not shut me out from life, do not wish me to be stillborn. Here is one who only longs to be God's; do not make a present of him to the world again, or delude him with the things of earth. Allow me to attain to light, light pure and undefiled; for only when I have come there shall I be truly a man. Leave me to imitate the passion of my God.

(Saint Ignatius of Antioch in a letter written on
his way to martyrdom)

51

My heart is open to you

Lord, I do not know what to ask of you. You alone know what are my true needs. You love me more than I myself know how to love. Help me to see my real needs which are concealed from me. I do not ask either a cross or a consolation; I can only wait for you. My heart is open to you. Visit and help me; cast me down and raise me up. I worship in silence your holy will and your inscrutable ways. I offer myself as a sacrifice to you. I put all my trust in you. I have no desire other than to fulfil your will. Teach me how to pray. Do you pray yourself in me. Amen.

(Philaret of Moscow)

Blessed are you, Lord God

Blessed are you, Lord, God of our ancestors, and worthy
    of praise;
and glorious is your name for ever.
For you are just in all you have done;
all your works are true and your ways right, and all your
    judgements are true.
For we have sinned and broken your law in turning
    away from you;
in all matters we have sinned grievously.
And now we cannot open our mouths;
We, your servants who worship you, have become a
    shame and a reproach.
For your name's sake do not give us up for ever, and
    do not annul your covenant.
Do not withdraw your mercy from us.
For we, Lord, have become fewer than any other nation,
and are brought low this day in all the world because
    of our sins.
Yet with a contrite heart and a humble spirit may we
    be accepted.
Such may our sacrifice be in your sight today, and may

we unreservedly follow you,
for no shame will come to those who trust in you.
And now with all our heart we follow you, we revere
    you and seek your presence.
Deliver us in accordance with your marvellous works,
    and bring glory to your name, Lord.
    (Adapted from Daniel 3.26–27, 29, 33–35, 37, 39–41, 43)

Blessing

May the blessing of almighty God, Father, Son and Holy Spirit,
come down upon us and remain with us always. Amen.

* * *

Reflections

The voice of the people is the voice of God.
> *(Vox populi, vox Dei: written by Alcuin in a
> letter to Charlemagne, AD 800)*

Every natural thing in its own way longs for the divine, and
desires to share in the divine life as far as it can.
> *(Aristotle)*

It is easier for a camel to go through the eye of a needle than for
someone who is rich to enter the kingdom of God.
> *(Mark 10.25)*

I offer you my actions

I adore you, my God, and I wish to love you with all my heart.
I thank you for having created me, made me a Christian, and
    kept me throughout the night.
I offer you my actions of this day; grant that they may be for
    my good and for your glory.
Keep me from sin and from all evil.
May your grace be always with me and with my dear ones.
Amen.

(Anon)

Do not send us away empty

Hear our voice, eternal God; have pity and compassion on us,
and receive our prayers with mercy and favour, for you are the
God who listens to prayers and petitions. Therefore, do not
send us away empty from your presence, our King, because in
your mercy you listen to the prayers of your people; for the
honour of your great Name. Amen.

(Daily Prayer of the Jews)

Single-minded and sincere

God, make me single-minded and sincere; take away all that is
not true, all that hinders your work in me; for only so shall I
serve you. Amen.

(Attributed to Saint Francis of Assisi)

Praise the Lord

Praise the Lord, all you nations,
acclaim him, all you peoples!
Strong is his love for us;
he is faithful for ever.

    (Adapted from Psalm 117)

Hail, holy queen

Hail, holy queen, mother of mercy; hail, our life, our sweetness, and our hope! To you do we cry, poor banished children of Eve! To you do we send up our sighs, mourning and weeping in this valley of tears! Turn, then, most gracious advocate, your eyes of mercy towards us, and, after this our exile, show unto us the blessed fruit of your womb, Jesus, O clement, O loving, O sweet virgin Mary.

(Adapted from Reichenau Abbey, Germany, about tenth century)

Angel guardian

My good angel, whom God has appointed to be my guardian,
  watch over me during this day.
Angels and saints of God, pray for me.
The Lord bless us and keep us from evil, and bring us to
  everlasting life. Amen.

(Anon)

* * *

Reflections

Christian, recognize your dignity, and, having been made a sharer in the divine nature, do not, through unworthy behaviour, return to the base ways of your past.

(Pope Saint Leo the Great)

Even fools who keep silent are considered wise; when they close their lips they are deemed intelligent.

(Proverbs 17.28)

In the virgin Mary, everything is relative to Christ and dependent upon him.

(Pope Paul VI, Marialis Cultus)

Glory to God

Glory to God in the highest, and peace to his people on earth.
Lord God, heavenly king, almighty God and Father;
we worship you, we give you thanks, we praise you for your
    glory.
Lord Jesus Christ, only Son of the Father, Lord God, Lamb
    of God,
you take away the sins of the world: have mercy on us;
you are seated at the right hand of the Father: receive our
    prayer.
For you alone are the Holy One, you alone are the Lord,
you alone are the Most High, Jesus Christ,
with the Holy Spirit, in the glory of God the Father. Amen.

(From the Roman liturgy)

Be near to the aged

Eternal Father, you who are unchanged down the changing
years, be near to the aged. Even though their bodies weaken,
grant that their spirit may be strong; may they bear weariness
and affliction with patience, and, at the end, meet death with
serenity; through Christ our Lord. Amen.

(Adapted from Pope Paul VI)

Overcome the temptations of this present world

Almighty God and Father, let your gracious and holy Spirit
descend upon us, so that no unchaste thought may corrupt the
souls which you have ordained for your praise, no unchaste
actions defile the bodies which are temples of the Holy Spirit.
Grant that, our hearts being filled with love of you, we may be
enabled to overcome the temptations of this present life, and
finally be made partakers of the glories of the world to come;
through Jesus Christ our Lord. Amen.

(Adapted from an Anglican source)

All that is pleasing to you

Give me grace, merciful God, to desire strongly all that is pleasing to you, to examine it carefully, to accept it truthfully, and to perform it generously, for the praise and glory of your name. Amen.

(Anon)

The faithful hands of God

Into the faithful hands of God we commit ourselves now and always. Lord, let us be yours and remain yours for ever; through Jesus Christ your Son our Lord. Amen.

(Weimarischer Gesangbuch)

Blessing

May God's grace be with us. Amen.

(Adapted from Colossians 4.18)

* * *

Reflections

Do not speak harshly to an older man, but speak to him as to a father, to younger men as brothers, to older women as mothers, to younger women as sisters – with absolute purity.

(1 Timothy 5.1–2)

In Calcutta there are homes for the dying. Those are visible buildings, but many young people in other countries find themselves in invisible homes for the dying. For their lives are characterized by abandonment, lack of affection or worry about their future. Broken relationships have wounded their innocence in childhood or adolescence. In some this leads to disillusionment, so that they ask: 'What is the use of living? Does life have any meaning?'

(Adapted from Mother Teresa of Calcutta)

Sacred Scripture will be recognized by all as the unfailing source of the spiritual life, the basis of all Christian instruction, and the very kernel of theological study.

(Pope Paul VI)

Let the peoples praise you, God

God, be gracious and bless us and let your face shed its light
upon us.
So will your ways be known upon earth and all nations
learn your saving help.
Let the peoples praise you, God; let all the peoples
praise you.
Let the nations be glad and exult, for you rule the world
with justice.
With fairness you rule the peoples, you guide the nations
on earth.
Let the peoples praise you, God; let all the peoples praise you.
The earth has yielded its fruit, for God, our God, has
blessed us.
May God still give us his blessing till the ends of the
earth revere him.
Let the peoples praise you, God; let all the peoples
praise you.

(Adapted from Psalm 67)

I now receive your beloved Son

Almighty and ever-living God, I approach the sacrament of
your only-begotten Son, our Lord Jesus Christ. I come sick to
the doctor of life, unclean to the fountain of mercy, blind to the
radiance of eternal light, poor and needy to the Lord of heaven
and earth. Lord, in your great generosity, heal my sickness, wash
away my defilement, enlighten my blindness, enrich my poverty,
and clothe my nakedness.

May I receive the bread of angels, the King of kings and Lord
of lords, with humble reverence, with purity and faith, repentance and love, and a determined purpose that will help to
bring me to salvation. May I receive the sacrament of the Lord's
body and blood, and its reality and power.

Loving God, may I receive the body of your only-begotten Son,
our Lord Jesus Christ, born from the womb of the virgin Mary,

and so be received into his mystical body and be numbered among his members.

Loving Father, as on my earthly pilgrimage I now receive your beloved Son under the sign of a sacrament, may I one day see him face to face in glory, who lives and reigns with you for ever and ever. Amen.

(Saint Thomas Aquinas)

Go to the Eucharist shoeless

Go to the Eucharist shoeless and make no show of your clothes. Go out in the name of the Trinity and greet twice over the poor, for the Son of God is disguised in them. No matter what you have seen of silver and gold, and heard of music on the harp, you will never see the kingdom of the Son of God without the blessing of the poor and alms to them.

(Adapted from the Celtic)

Holy Trinity

Father, my hope; Son, my refuge; Holy Spirit, my protection; Holy Trinity, glory be to you. Amen.

(Saint Ioanniki)

* * *

Reflections

Before people can come to the liturgy, they must be called to faith and conversion.

(Vatican II, Sacrosanctum Concilium)

The reception of Christ's body and blood does nothing less than transform us into that which we consume, and henceforth we bear in soul and body him in whose friendship we died, were buried and are risen again.

(Pope Saint Leo the Great)

Jesus said to them, 'Come away to a deserted place all by yourselves and rest a while.'

(Mark 6.31)

Persevere with steadfast faith

Almighty and everlasting God, who has revealed your glory among the nations through Jesus Christ, preserve the works of your mercy, so that your people, spread throughout the world, may persevere with steadfast faith in the profession of your name; through Jesus Christ our Lord. Amen.

(Gelasian Sacramentary)

Generosity to follow your call

Jesus, Son of the eternal Father and of Mary, grant to men and women the generosity necessary to follow your call, and the courage to overcome all obstacles to their vocation. Give to families that faith, love and spirit of sacrifice which will inspire them to encourage each other to rejoice whenever one of them is called to your service in the priesthood, religious life or in any special way. Let your example, and that of your mother and Saint Joseph, encourage Christian families, and let your grace sustain them. Amen.

(Anon)

Bless farmers

Almighty God, you crown the year with your goodness. We ask you to bless with your generosity the farmers and workers on the land, that, as they sow in hope, they may also in due time gather in the harvest with joy; through Jesus Christ our Lord. Amen.

(Adapted from an Anglican source)

Our eternal heritage

Lord God, stand by your people on whom you have bestowed the gift of faith. Grant us our eternal heritage in the resurrection of your only Son; through Christ our Lord. Amen.

(Adapted from the Roman liturgy)

Christ, Son of the living God

Christ, Son of the living God, may your holy angels guard our sleep. May they watch over us while we rest and hover around our beds.

Let them reveal to us in our dreams visions of your glorious truth, high prince of the universe, high priest of the mysteries. May no dreams disturb our rest, and no nightmares darken our dreams. May no fears or worries delay our willing, prompt repose.

May the virtue of our daily work hallow our nightly prayers. May our sleep be deep and soft so that our work be fresh and hard.

(Celtic; attributed to Saint Patrick)

Doxology

To the only God our Saviour, through Jesus Christ our Lord, be glory, majesty, power and authority, before all time, now and for ever. Amen.

(Adapted from Jude 25)

* * *

Reflections

The particular discovery that modern man is making . . . is that reality can be known only as a whole, not in parts, and that this total apprehension can be realized only in silence.

(John Main)

Now the word of the Lord came to me saying, 'Before I formed you in the womb I knew you, and before you were born I consecrated you; I appointed you a prophet to the nations.' Then I said, 'Ah, Lord God! Truly I do not know how to speak, for I am only a child.' But the Lord said to me, 'Do not say, "I am only a child"; for you shall go to all to whom I send you, and you shall speak whatever I command you. Do not be afraid of them, for I am with you to deliver you,' says the Lord.

(Adapted from Jeremiah 1.4–8)

In heaven we shall be at rest and we shall see God; our eyes will feast on him and our hearts will overflow with love; our hearts will overflow with love and we shall praise him – and that will have no end.

(Saint Augustine)

61

Be a rock of refuge for me

In you, Lord, I take refuge. Let me never be put to shame.
In your justice, set me free, hear me and speedily rescue me.
Be a rock of refuge for me, a mighty stronghold to save me.
For you are my rock, my stronghold; for your name's sake,
　　lead me and guide me.
Release me from the snares they have hidden, for you are
　　my refuge, Lord.
Into your hands, I commend my spirit. It is you who will
　　redeem me, Lord.

(Adapted from Psalm 31)

Seeking Christ in prayer

Christ my Lord, again and again I have said with Mary
Magdalene, 'They have taken away my Lord and I don't know
where they have put him.' I have been desolate and alone. And
you have found me again, and I know that what has died is not
you, Lord, but only my idea of you, the image I made to preserve
what I found, and to be my security. I will make another image,
Lord, better than the last. That, too, must go, and all successive
images, until I come to the blessed vision of yourself, Christ my
Lord. Amen.

(George Appleton)

Let us go forth

Let us go forth
in the goodness of our merciful Father, in the gentleness of
　　our brother Jesus,
in the radiance of his Holy Spirit, in the faith of the apostles,
in the joyful praise of the angels, in the holiness of the saints,
　　in the courage of the martyrs.
Let us go forth
in the wisdom of our all-seeing Father, in the patience of
　　our all-loving brother,

in the truth of the all-knowing Spirit, in the learning of the
   apostles,
in the gracious guidance of the angels, in the patience of the
   saints, in the self-control of the martyrs.
Such is the path for all servants of Christ, the path from
   death to eternal life.

(Celtic; attributed to Saint Patrick)

Help me to do the work

Lord Jesus Christ, only Son of the Father, you have said to us,
'Without me you can do nothing.' Lord, my Lord, with faith I
embrace in my heart and soul the words you have spoken.
Although I am a sinner, help me to do the work begun by me
for your sake, in the name of the Father, and of the Son, and of
the Holy Spirit. Amen.

(Orthodox)

* * *

Reflections

When Peter noticed the strong wind, he became frightened,
and, beginning to sink, he cried out, 'Lord, save me!' Jesus
immediately reached out his hand and caught him, saying to
him, 'You of little faith, why did you doubt?'

(Adapted from Matthew 14.30–31)

Politics without principle, wealth without work, commerce
without morality, pleasure without conscience, education without character, science without humanity and worship without
sacrifice.

(The Seven Social Sins, according to Mahatma Gandhi)

If you have lost the taste for prayer, you will regain the desire
for it by returning to its practice. Do not forget the evidence of
history: faithfulness to prayer or its abandonment are the test
of the vitality or the decadence of the Christian life.

(Adapted from Pope Paul VI)

Direct our thoughts and actions

Father, you are the author of all good things; work powerfully in us your servants so that we may do good to all, and be channels of your mercy and grace. Lead us, and direct our thoughts and actions so that we may serve you in justice and holiness. Sanctify us all unto eternal life which we, with all your creatures, working and struggling together, wait for and expect; through Jesus Christ our Lord. Amen.

(Adapted from Philip Melanchton)

For governments

Enlighten all governments to uphold standards of right and wrong, and so help to dispel the darkness of sin from your creation. Guide national leaders to establish the rule of justice and peace for the whole human family. Amen.

(Anon)

I want to unite myself to you

Jesus, I want to unite myself to you and to possess you, so that I no longer live except for you who will be my dwelling-place for eternity. In you, Jesus, I desire to love and work and suffer. Take away from me all that is of self. In its place put your self; change me so as to be like you. May I no longer live except by you and for you. Be, therefore, my life, my love, my all.

(Margaret Mary Alacoque)

We may always seek your face

Almighty and merciful God, the fountain of all goodness, who knows the thoughts of hearts, we confess to you that we have sinned against you and done evil in your sight. Wash us from the stains of our sins, and give us grace and power to put away all hurtful things so that, being freed from the slavery which is sin, we may be free for a new life in you.

Eternal light, shine into our hearts. Eternal goodness, deliver us from evil. Eternal power, be our support. Eternal wisdom, scatter the darkness of our ignorance. Eternal pity, have mercy on us. Grant us, that with our heart and mind and strength, we may always seek your face, and finally bring us in your infinite mercy to your holy presence. Strengthen our weakness so that, following in the footsteps of your blessed Son, we may obtain your mercy and enter into your promised joy; through the same Christ our Lord. Amen.

(Adapted from Alcuin)

Blessing

May the God of peace sanctify us entirely; and may our spirit, and soul, and body, be kept sound and blameless at the coming of our Lord Jesus Christ. The one who calls us is faithful, and will do this. Amen.

(Adapted from 1 Thessalonians 5.23–24)

* * *

Reflections

What are you looking for?

(John 1.38)

They who sing the song of loyalty to their earthly country must not become deserters and traitors in disloyalty to their God, their church, and their heavenly country.

(Pope Pius XI, Mit brennender Sorge)

Knowing God without knowing our own weakness makes for pride.

(Blaise Pascal)

May I seek you

May I seek you, Lord, by praying to you, and let me pray to you by believing in you.

(Saint Augustine)

We give you thanks

We give you thanks, yes, more than thanks, Lord our God, for all your goodness at all times and in all places, because you have shielded, rescued, helped and guided us all the days of our lives, and brought us to this hour. We pray and beseech you, merciful God, to grant, in your goodness, that we may spend this day and all the days of our life, without sin, in fullness of joy, holiness and reverence for you. Drive away from us, Lord, all envy, fear and temptation. Give us what is good and just. Whatever sin we commit in thought, word or deed, pardon us in your goodness and mercy. And lead us not into temptation, but deliver us from evil; through the grace, mercy and love of your only Son, Jesus Christ our Lord. Amen.

(Adapted from the liturgy of Saint Mark)

Make us complete

Almighty Father, God of peace, you brought back from the dead our Lord Jesus, the great Shepherd of the sheep; make us complete in everything good so that we may do his will, and work in us that which is pleasing in your sight; through Jesus Christ to whom be the glory forever and ever. Amen.

(Adapted from Hebrews 13.20–21)

Loyalty to the faith

Almighty God, who show to those who are in error the light of truth so that they may return to the ways of justice, grant to all who are admitted into the communion of saints, that they may renounce all that is contrary to the faith, and follow all that is in keeping with it; through our Lord Jesus Christ. Amen.

(Adapted from the Leonine Sacramentary)

Receive your word with reverence and humility
Lord, heavenly Father, in whom is the fullness of light and wisdom, enlighten our minds by your Holy Spirit, and give us grace to receive your word with reverence and humility, without which no one can understand your truth; for Jesus Christ's sake. Amen.

(John Calvin)

Heal the sick
Lord, comfort all who are ill in body, soul or mind. Heal them as you will. Bless the work of doctors, and nurses, and all those who support them. May they join caring to curing in the service of those who are weak and suffering. May they never tire of being compassionate but persevere in their efforts to relieve the pain of humanity. We ask this in Jesus' name. Amen.

(Anon)

* * *

Reflections

I still have many things to say to you, but you cannot bear them now. When the Spirit of truth comes, he will guide you into all the truth.

(John 16.12–13)

One thing you may be sure of, that while you work for God, whether you succeed or not, he will amply reward you.

(Edmund Ignatius Rice)

Love ought to manifest itself more by deeds than by words.

(Ignatius Loyola)

Break down the walls which divide us

Lord God, you have created the earth from end to end, and in you there is no distinction of race, colour, class or language, but in you all are one. We ask you to break down the walls which divide us so that we may work together with one mind and heart, with one another and with you. We ask this in Jesus' name. Amen.

(Adapted from an Anglican source)

Lord, help me

Lord, help me to live this evening, quietly, easily;
to lean on your great strength, trustfully, restfully;
to wait for the unfolding of your will, patiently, serenely;
to meet others, peacefully, joyfully;
to face tomorrow, confidently, courageously. Amen.

(Anon)

For someone who is dying

In the name of God the Father who created you, in the name of Jesus Christ, Son of the living God, who suffered for you, in the name of the Holy Spirit, who was poured out upon you, go forth, faithful Christian. May you live in peace this day, may your home be with God, with Mary the virgin mother of God, with Joseph and all the angels and saints.

My sister (brother) in faith, (*name*), I entrust you to God who created you. May you return to the One who formed you from the dust of this earth. May Mary, the angels, and all the saints come to meet you as you go forth from this life. May Christ who was crucified for you bring you freedom and peace. May Christ, the Son of God, who died for you, take you into his kingdom. May Christ, the good shepherd, give you a place in his flock. May he forgive your sins and keep you among his people. May you see your Redeemer face to face and enjoy the sight of God for ever.

Lord Jesus Christ, Saviour of the world, we commend your servant, (*name*), to you and pray for her (him). In mercy you came to earth for her (his) sake: accept her (him) into the joy of your kingdom. Though she (he) has failed and sinned, she (he) has not denied the Father, the Son and the Holy Spirit, but has believed and worshipped God the Creator: accept her (him) into the joy of your kingdom. Amen.

(Adapted from the Roman liturgy)

Remember me, Lord

Remember, your mercy, Lord, and the love you have shown
    from of old.
Do not remember the sins of my youth. In your love
    remember me.

(Adapted from Psalm 25)

Blessing

May the God of infinite goodness scatter the darkness of sin and brighten our hearts with holiness. Amen.

(Adapted from the Roman liturgy)

* * *

Reflections

What do you want me to do for you?

(Luke 18.41)

Considering the omnipotence and mercy of God, no one should despair of the salvation of anyone in this life.

(Saint Thomas Aquinas)

To speak of the divine will is not to speak of what God wants – it is to speak of what he is. What is the divine will? It is, simply, love.

(Adapted from John Main)

Another day

I thank you, Lord, for the wonder of my being, for giving me another day to love and serve you. May I often think of you during it! Inspire everything that I say and do this day. May it all begin from you and, with your unfailing help, be carried through for your glory; through Christ our Lord. Amen.

(Adapted from the Catholic Truth Society)

Open our hearts

Lord, open our hearts to your grace. Restrain us from all human waywardness, and keep us faithful to your commandments; through Christ our Lord. Amen.

(Adapted from the Roman liturgy)

Saint Joseph's example

Lord God and Creator of the universe, you imposed the law of work on the human race. Give us grace, by Saint Joseph's example and at his intercession, to finish the works you give us to do, and come to the rewards you promise; through Christ our Lord. Amen.

(Adapted from the Roman liturgy)

God be with me

God be in my head and in my understanding.
God be in my eyes and in my looking.
God be in my mouth and in my speaking.
God be in my heart and in my thinking.
God be at my end and at my departing.

(Sarum Primer)

Teach me to be generous

Lord Jesus, teach me to be generous, to serve you as you deserve to be served; to give without counting the cost; to fight without heeding the wounds; to work without seeking for rest; to spend

my life without expecting any return other than the knowledge
that I do your holy will. Amen.

(Ignatius Loyola)

God alone is sufficient

Let nothing disturb you, nothing frighten you.
All things are passing, God never changes.
Patient endurance attains to all things.
Whom God possesses, in nothing is wanting.
God alone suffices.

(Teresa of Avila)

* * *

Reflections

Do not say, 'It was the Lord's doing that I fell away'; for he does
not do what he hates. Do not say, 'It was he who led me astray';
for he has no need of the sinful. The Lord hates all abomina-
tions; such things are not loved by those who revere him. It was
he who created humankind in the beginning, and he left them
in the power of their own free choice. If you choose, you can
keep the commandments, and to act faithfully is a matter of
your own choice. He has placed before you fire and water;
stretch out your hand to whichever you choose. Before each
person are life and death, and whichever one chooses will be
given. For great is the wisdom of the Lord; he is mighty in
power and sees everything; his eyes are on those who revere
him, and he knows every human action. He has not commanded
anyone to be wicked, and he has not given anyone permission
to sin.

(Adapted from Sirach 15.11–20)

Where does God live? Wherever a heart and mind let him.

(Jewish tradition)

He who does not bellow the truth when he knows the truth
makes himself the accomplice of liars and forgers.

(Charles Péguy)

Free me from falsehood

Lord my God, hear my prayer: in your mercy answer my request; it is not just for myself, but I make it for others too. You see into my heart and you know that it is so. Let me offer you my mind and tongue in your service, if you will give me the means of making such an offering. I am poor and in need, but you richly bless all who call to you. You who are free from care, care for us. Free my mind and my heart from all falsehood. Let my yes be yes, and my no be no.

(Adapted from Saint Augustine)

You have made me for joy

As the hand is made for holding and the eye for seeing, you have made me for joy. Share with me the vision that shall find it everywhere: in the wild violet's beauty; in the lark's melody; in the face of a steadfast person; in a child's smile; in a mother's love; in the purity of Jesus. Amen.

(Celtic)

The God of gifts, the gifts of God

God who made me is good, and is my own good. I rejoice in his goodness which, even in childhood, filled my own existence. I thank you in whom I place my confidence and my trust. I thank you, loving God, for all your gifts, and ask you to keep them for me.

(Adapted from Saint Augustine)

The Spirit of the Lord

May the Spirit of the Lord rest on us: the Spirit of wisdom and understanding, the Spirit of counsel and might, the Spirit of knowledge and reverence for the Lord. May our delight be to revere the Lord who does not judge by what his eyes see, or decide by what his ears hear, but who judges with justice.

(Adapted from Isaiah 11.2–3)

Peace and unity

Lord Jesus Christ, you said to your apostles: I leave you peace, my peace I give you. Look not on our sins, but on the faith of your church, and grant us the peace and unity of your kingdom where you live for ever and ever.

(Adapted from the Roman liturgy)

Blessing

May the God of all grace, who calls us to his eternal glory in Christ, restore, support, strengthen and establish us. To him be the power for ever and ever. Amen.

(Adapted from 1 Peter 5.10–11)

* * *

Reflections

Do you believe that I am able to do this?

(Matthew 9.28)

A person who has lost a sense of wonder is already dead.

(William of Saint Thierry)

Always accept the truth about yourself . . . however beautiful it may be.

(Anon)

God the true and supreme good

Let us desire nothing else, let us wish for nothing else, let nothing else please us and cause us delight, except our Creator and Redeemer and Saviour, the one true God, who is fullness of good, all good, every good, the true and supreme good, who alone is holy, just and true, holy and right, who alone is kind, innocent and pure; from whom and through whom and in whom is all pardon, all grace and all glory. Amen.

(Saint Francis of Assisi)

Praise of God's love

Lord, you loved me from all eternity, therefore you
    created me.
You loved me after you had made me, therefore you
    became man for me.
You loved me after you became man for me, therefore
    you lived and died for me.
You loved me after you had died for me, therefore you
    rose again for me.
You loved me after you had risen for me, therefore you
    went to prepare a place for me.
You loved me after you had gone to prepare a place for
    me, therefore you came back to me.
You loved me after you had come back to me, therefore
    you desire to enter into me and be united with me.
This is the meaning of the Blessed Sacrament, the
    mystery of love. Amen.

(Alban Goodier)

One communion

Lord Jesus Christ, when you were about to suffer, you prayed for your disciples to the end of time, that they might all be one as you are in the Father and the Father in you. Look down in pity on the many divisions among those who profess your faith, and heal the wounds which human pride has inflicted on your people. Break down the walls of separation which divide one party and denomination of Christians from another. Look with compassion on the souls of those who have been born in one or another of these various denominations, and bring them all into that one communion which you willed from the beginning.

(Adapted from John Henry Newman)

Accept the praises we offer you

Lord our God, who have subjected all rational and spiritual powers to your will, we pray and beseech you to accept the praises we offer you as well as we are able, together with all creation, and we ask that you will give us all the riches of your goodness; before you every knee shall bow, in heaven and on earth and under the earth: all things living and created praise your unfathomable glory, you who are the one true God, abounding in mercy. With all the powers of heaven we praise and glorify you, Father, Son and Holy Spirit, now and for ever, to the ages of ages. Amen.

(Orthodox)

* * *

Reflections

The essence of religion is to become like him whom you worship.

(Saint Augustine)

Make every effort to maintain the unity of the Spirit in the bond of peace. There is one body and one Spirit, just as you were called to the one hope of your calling, one Lord, one faith, one baptism, one God and Father of all, who is above all and through all and in all.

(Adapted from Ephesians 4.3–6)

The heart has reasons of its own, of which reason knows nothing.

(Blaise Pascal)

Acts of faith, hope and love

My God, I believe in you and in all that you teach, because
you have said it, and your word is true.

My God, I hope in you, for grace and for glory, because of
your promises, your mercy and your power.

My God, because you are so good, I want to love you with
all my heart, and for your sake to love my neighbour as
myself. Amen.

(Anon)

I want to have confidence in your love

My God, I want to have confidence in your love, but so many
things seem to hold me back: past wounds, past hurts, past
betrayals, past sins – mine and others'. Open my eyes. Open my
heart. Enable me to take the leap of faith that is needed now.
Holiness isn't a matter of starting to love you some time in the
future, or even tomorrow. I don't have to wait until I become a
better person, more worthy, more virtuous. It's a matter of
trusting in your mercy *today*, just as I am. You showed this to
the saints; show me, too, and give me a spirit of great confidence. I ask this through your beloved Son, our merciful
Saviour. Amen.

(Elizabeth Ruth Obbard)

Faithful stewards of wealth

Lord God, whose blessed Son Jesus Christ taught us that all
things we possess are committed to us in trust from you, help
us to be faithful stewards of the wealth which you have committed to us, so that in earning we may be just and honourable,
and in spending we may seek first not our own selfish interest
but the good of others; through the same Christ our Lord.
Amen.

(Adapted from an Anglican source)

Teach me what you want me to do

Listen to me, Lord, and answer me for I am helpless and weak. Save me from death. You are my God; be merciful to me, I ask you all the day long. You are good and forgiving, full of constant love for all who pray to you. Listen, Lord, to my prayer; hear my cries for help. I call on you in times of trouble, because you answer my prayers. Teach me, Lord, what you want me to do, and I will obey you faithfully.

(Anon)

Holy, holy, holy

Holy, holy, holy, the Lord God the almighty who was and is
    and is to come.
You are worthy, our Lord and God, to receive glory and
    honour and power,
for you created all things and by your will they existed
    and were created.

(Adapted from Revelation 4.8, 11)

* * *

Reflections

Do you believe in the Son of Man?

(John 9.35)

We need to trust in God as if everything depended on him, and, at the same time, to work generously as if everything depended on us.

(Post-Vatican II documents)

There's nothing enlightened about shrinking so that other people won't feel insecure around us. We were born to manifest the glory of God that is within us. It's not just in some of us; it's in everyone. And as we let our own light shine we unconsciously give other people permission to do the same. As we were liberated from our own fear, our presence automatically liberates others.

(Nelson Mandela)

Trust in God's protection

You who dwell in the shelter of the Most High, and abide in
   the shade of the Almighty
will say to the Lord, 'My refuge, my stronghold, my God in
   whom I trust!'
You who have said, 'Lord, my refuge!' and have made the
   Most High your dwelling,
upon you no evil shall fall, no plague approach where you
   dwell.
For you has he commanded his angels, to keep you in all
   your ways.
They shall bear you upon their hands lest you strike
   your foot against a stone.
Those who love me, I will deliver; I will protect those who
   know my name.
When they call, I shall answer: 'I am with you'.
I will save them in distress and give them glory.
With length of life I will content them;
I shall let them see my saving power.

(Adapted from Psalm 91)

Remember the poor

Remember the poor when you look out on the fields you own,
   on your plump cows.
Remember the poor when you look into your barn, at the
   abundance of your harvest.
Remember the poor when the wind howls and the rain falls,
   as you sit warm and dry in your house.
Remember the poor when you eat fine meat and drink fine
   ale at your fine carved table.
The cows have grass to eat, the rabbits have burrows for
   shelter, the birds have warm nests.

But the poor have no food except when you feed them, no
shelter except your house when you welcome them,
no warmth except your glowing fire.

(Adapted from the Celtic)

I abandon myself

Father, I abandon myself into your hands; do with me as
you will.
For whatever you do, I thank you; I am ready for all, I
accept all.
Let your will be done in me as in all creatures; I ask
nothing else.
Into your hands I commend my soul; I give it to you with
all the love of my heart.
I love you and I want to give myself into your hands with
a trust beyond all measure because you are my Father.
Amen.

(Charles de Foucauld)

* * *

Reflections

Jesus is able for all time to save those who approach God
through him, since he always lives to make intercession for
them.

(Adapted from Hebrews 7.25)

The one who prays will certainly be saved.

(Alphonsus Liguori)

Jesus, compel us to discard our pettiness and to venture forth,
resting upon you, into the uncharted ocean of your love.

(Teilhard de Chardin)

Have mercy on me, God

Have mercy on me, God, in your kindness; in your
  compassion blot out my offence.
Wash me more and more from my guilt and cleanse
  me from my sin.
My offences truly I know them; my sin is always before me.
Against you, you alone, have I sinned; what is evil in your
  sight I have done.
Indeed you love truth in the heart; then in the secret of
  my heart teach me wisdom.
Purify me, then I shall be clean; wash me, I shall be whiter
  than snow.
Make me hear rejoicing and gladness, that the bones you
  have crushed may revive.
From my sins turn away your face and blot out all my guilt.
A pure heart create for me, God, and put a steadfast spirit
  within me.
Do not cast me away from your presence, nor deprive me
  of your Holy Spirit.
Give me again the joy of your help; with a spirit of fervour
  sustain me
that I may teach transgressors your ways and sinners may
  return to you.
Rescue me, God my helper, and my tongue shall ring out
  your goodness.
Lord, open my lips and my mouth shall declare your praise.
For in sacrifice you take no delight, burnt offering from me
  you would refuse;
my sacrifice, a contrite spirit. A humbled, contrite heart
  you will not spurn.

(Adapted from Psalm 51)

Angel sent by God

Angel sent by God to guide me, be my light and walk beside me.

Be my guardian and protect me; on the paths of life direct me. Amen.

(Anon)

To wait and to watch

Help us, Lord, always to wait for you and to watch for you, so that at your coming again, you may find us ready. We ask this for your Name's sake. Amen.

(Adapted from an ancient Collect)

Blessing

May God the Father and the Lord Jesus Christ give peace to the whole community and love with faith.

(Adapted from Ephesians 6.23)

* * *

Reflections

Do you now believe?

(John 16.31)

Take time to think: it is the source of power.
Take time to play: it is the secret of perpetual youth.
Take time to read: it is the fountain of wisdom.
Take time to pray: it is the greatest power on earth.
Take time to love and to be loved: it is a God-given privilege.
Take time to be friendly: it is the road to happiness.
Take time to laugh: it is the music of the soul.
Take time to give: it is too short a day to be selfish.
Take time to work: it is the price of success.
Take time to do charity: it is the key to heaven.

(Anon)

Compassion is the shaping principle of the human and of the Christian.

(Jon Sobrino)

I give you my whole self

Lord Jesus, I give you my hands to do your work. I give you my feet to go your way.

I give you my eyes to see as you see. I give you my tongue to speak your words.

I give you my mind that you may think in me. I give you my spirit that you may pray in me.

Above all, I give you my heart that you may love in me – love the Father and all humanity.

I give you my whole self that you may grow in me, so that you, Lord, may be the one who lives, and works, and prays in me. Amen.

(Congregation of the Most Holy Redeemer)

Prayer for a friend

Lord Jesus, give (*name*) a heart to love you, a will to choose you, a memory to remember you, a mind to think of you, a soul which may always be united to you. And may you, the God of love and mercy, love (*name*) for ever. Amen.

(Saint Augustine)

New heaven and new earth

Then I saw a new heaven and a new earth . . . And I saw the holy city, the new Jerusalem, coming down out of heaven from God, prepared as a bride adorned for her husband. And I heard a loud voice from the throne saying, 'See, the home of God is among mortals. He will dwell with them as their God; and they will be his peoples, and God himself will be with them; he will wipe away every tear from their eyes. Death will be no more; mourning and crying and pain will be no more, for the first things have passed away.' And the one who was seated on the throne said, 'See, I am making all things new.'

(Revelation 21.1–5)

Time for things

God, keep me from smallness of mind. Let me be big in thought, word and action. Let me be finished for ever with self-love and fault-finding. May I put away all pretence, and meet everyone face to face without self-pity or deceit. May I not be hasty in judging others, but may I always be generous. Let me take time for things. Help me grow calm, peaceful and gentle. Teach me to put my good intentions into action. Teach me to be straightforward and fearless. Grant that I may realize that it is the small things in life that separate us, and that in the big things of life we are one. Amen.

(Anon)

Lord, I believe

Lord, I believe with joy all that is named from of old in the creeds of the gentle apostles. I believe completely because, in your lifetime, you really revealed them to us. Every moment of my life I believe in my heart in one God in three persons, the bright eternal Father, the most holy Son of peace, and the Holy Spirit who came from them both.

(Pádraig Ó Callanáin)

* * *

Reflections

Serve one another with whatever gift each of you has received.
(1 Peter 4.10b)

Our Lord does not ask for great achievements, only for self-surrender, and for gratitude.
(Thérèse of Lisieux)

The terrible experience of being apparently without faith in order to grow in faith.
(Thomas Merton)

Hail, Mary

Hail, Mary, full of grace, the Lord is with you! Blessed are you among women, and blessed is the fruit of your womb, Jesus. Holy Mary, Mother of God, pray for us sinners now and at the hour of our death. Amen.

(Adapted from Luke 1.27–31, 42)

Deliver us, Lord

Deliver us, Lord, from every evil and grant us peace in our day. In your mercy keep us free from sin, and protect us from all anxiety, as we wait in joyful hope for the coming of our Saviour, Jesus Christ.

(Adapted from the Roman liturgy)

The gifts of God

Most holy God, we pray and beseech you, give each of us a pure heart and a way of speaking that befits the faith we profess; grant us uprightness of purpose, powers of reasoning unhindered by passions, conduct appropriate to those who venerate you, and full knowledge of your commandments. May we enjoy health in body and in spirit. Grant us a life of peace, genuine faith and living hope, sincere charity and bountiful generosity, patience that knows no bounds and the light of your truth to proclaim your goodness to us, so that for ever and in all things placing our trust in you, we may abound in every good work, and that, in Christ, your gifts may increase in every soul. For to you belong all glory, honour and majesty, Father, Son, and Holy Spirit, now and for ever, to the ages of ages. Amen.

(Orthodox)

Open to your word

Almighty Father, your constant love has been handed down to us in human words through the work of others. Help us to be quiet, and to be open to your word when it is proclaimed to us in the Scriptures this day and every day.

(Anon)

Be present with us

Almighty and everlasting God, be present with us in all our duties, and grant the protection of your presence to all who live in this house, so that you may be known to be the defender of this household and the inhabitant of this house; through Jesus Christ our Lord. Amen.

(Gelasian Sacramentary)

Blessing

May our Lord bless us and keep us from all evil, and bring us to everlasting life. Amen.

(Adapted from the Roman liturgy)

* * *

Reflections

Do you have eyes and fail to see?

(Mark 8.18)

What the soul has to do is nothing more than to be gentle and without noise. By noise, I mean going about with the understanding in search of words and reflections whereby to give God thanks for his grace, and heaping up its sins and imperfections together to show that it does not deserve it. Let it simply say words of love that suggest themselves immediately, firmly grounded in the conviction that what it says is true.

(Teresa of Avila)

To pray often is in your will, but to pray truly is a gift of grace.

(Saint Makarios the Great)

Christ Jesus

Though he was in the form of God,
[Jesus] did not regard equality with God
as something to be exploited,
but emptied himself,
taking the form of a slave,
being born in human likeness.
And being found in human form,
he humbled himself
and became obedient to the point of death –
even death on a cross.
Therefore God also highly exalted him
and gave him the name
that is above every name,
so that at the name of Jesus
every knee should bend,
in heaven and on earth and under the earth,
and every tongue should confess
that Jesus Christ is Lord,
to the glory of God the Father.

(Philippians 2.6–11)

The way to eternal life

God our Father, by raising Christ your Son you conquered the power of death and opened for us the way to eternal life. Let our celebration today of the resurrection of Jesus raise us up and renew our lives by the Spirit that is within us. We ask this through the same Christ our Lord. Amen.

(Adapted from the Roman liturgy)

I approach your holy table

Lord Jesus Christ, I approach your holy table in fear and trembling, for I am a sinner and dare not rely on my own worth but only on your goodness and mercy. I am defiled by many sins in body and soul, and by my unguarded thoughts and words.

Gracious God of majesty and awe, I seek your protection, I look for your healing. Sinner that I am, I appeal to you, the fountain of all mercy. I cannot bear your judgement, but I trust in your salvation. Lord, I show my wounds to you and uncover my shame before you. I know my sins are many and great, and they fill me with fear, but I hope in your mercies, for they cannot be numbered.

Lord Jesus Christ, eternal king, divine and human, crucified for humanity, look upon me with mercy and hear my prayer, for I trust in you. Have mercy on me, for the depth of your compassion never ends. Praise to you, saving sacrifice, offered on the wood of the cross for me and for all. Praise to the noble and precious blood, flowing from your wounds and washing away the sins of the whole world.

Remember, Lord, your creature, whom you have redeemed with your blood.

Merciful Lord, take away all my offences and sins; purify me in body and soul, and make me worthy to taste the holy of holies. May your body and blood, which I intend to receive, be for me the washing away of my guilt, and the rebirth of my better instincts. May it spur me on to works pleasing to you and be beneficial to my health in body and soul. Amen.

(Attributed to Saint Ambrose)

* * *

Reflections

God is not to be bargained with. We must give ourselves up to him unconditionally. Give him everything.

(Georges Bernanos)

Christ, by whom the church lives, is immeasurably greater than she imagines.

(Teilhard de Chardin)

Prayer with fasting is good, but better than both is almsgiving with justice. A little with justice is better than wealth with wrongdoing. It is better to give alms than to lay up gold. For almsgiving saves from death and purges away every sin.

(Adapted from Tobit 12.8–9)

Raise us up

God our Father, by raising Christ your Son you conquered the power of death and opened for us the way to eternal life. Let our prayers today raise us up and renew our lives by the Spirit that is within us. We make this prayer through Christ our Lord. Amen.

(Adapted from the Roman liturgy)

You were a friend

Jesus, you stood to be baptized with sinners at the Jordan; as one of them you fasted in the desert; as one of them you were tempted. You were a friend to the timid Nicodemus. You were a friend to the Samaritan woman, telling her of her sins, making confession for her. You were a friend to her friends. You called to yourself the sinner Levi; you dined with him and his friends until self-respecting people were scandalized, saying, 'Why does he dine with publicans and sinners?' You were a friend to Mary Magdalen, saying of her, 'Many sins are forgiven her because she loved much,' and saying to her 'Go in peace; your faith has made you safe.' You were a friend to the adulteress, shaming her accusers, saying 'Neither will I accuse; go now and sin no more.' You were a friend to the rich man who refused to follow you; you looked on him and loved him. You were a friend to the publican Zacchaeus, choosing to stay at his home. You were a friend to Judas who betrayed you, calling him by his name, calling him 'Friend'. You were a friend to Peter who denied you. You were a friend to Pilate who condemned you. You were a friend to the thief who cursed you, winning him to grace, saying to him, 'This day you will be with me in paradise.' You were a friend to all people, saying to them, 'Come to me all you who labour and are overburdened, and I will give you rest.'

(Alban Goodier)

Act of sorrow for sin

My God, I am heartily sorry for having offended you and I detest all my sins because they offend you, my God, who are all good and deserving of all my love. I firmly resolve, with the help of your grace, to sin no more and to avoid the occasions of sin.

(Anon)

Bless the efforts of your servants

Lord Jesus Christ, who was born in a stable and had nowhere to lay your head, bless the efforts of your servants to give homes to the homeless, work to the workless, and hope to the hopeless; who live and reign with the Father and the Holy Spirit, one God, forever and ever. Amen.

(Adapted from an Anglican source)

Blessing

The grace of our Lord Jesus Christ, the love of God, and the communion of the Holy Spirit be with all of us. Amen.

(Adapted from 2 Corinthians 13.13)

* * *

Reflections

Who do people say that I am?

(Mark 8.27)

We ourselves are the church, we poor, primitive, cowardly people, and together we represent the church. If we look at the church from the outside, as it were, then we have not grasped that we are the church.

(Karl Rahner)

Were we to know the merit of only going from one street to another to serve a neighbour for the love of God, we should prize it more than gold or silver.

(Edmund Ignatius Rice)

Make me able to pray

Make me, my God, self-controlled and alert, to be able to pray.

(Adapted from 1 Peter 4.7)

Fill us with your mercy

In this hour of this day, fill us, Lord, with your mercy, so that rejoicing throughout the whole day, we may take delight in your praise; through Jesus Christ our Lord. Amen.

(Sarum Breviary)

Give us a favourable hearing

God of mercy, shed your light on hearts that have been purified by penance, and in your goodness give us a favourable hearing when you move us to pray. We ask this through Christ our Lord. Amen.

(Adapted from the Roman liturgy)

Our Father

Deliver us from evil and lead us not into temptation. Forgive us our trespasses as we forgive those who trespass against us. Give us this day our daily bread. Your will be done on earth as it is in heaven. Your kingdom come. Hallowed be your name, our Father who art in heaven.

(Russian Orthodox)

Keep me from grumbling

God, keep me from grumbling. I know that there are few people harder to put up with than those who are always complaining. Don't let me become like that. Don't let me have discontent written all over my face. If I can't get my own way, don't let me sulk about it. If I can't get what I want, help me to make the best of what I have. Don't let me take offence easily, getting into a huff, even when no harm was intended. Help me all day and every day to see the best in people. Help me, too, to live in the certainty that you are working all things together for good. May I have the patience to wait for your purposes to work out. This I ask for your love's sake. Amen.

(Adapted from William Barclay)

Discerning the signs of the kingdom

Lord God, who set before us the great hope that your kingdom shall come on earth and taught us to pray for its coming: give us grace to discern the signs of its dawning and to work for the perfect day when the world shall reflect your glory; through Jesus Christ our Lord. Amen.

(Society of Saint Francis)

Keep us in your love

God our Father, in restoring our human nature from sin, you have given us a greater dignity than we had in the beginning. Keep us in your love, and continue to sustain those who have received the new life of baptism. We make this prayer through Christ our Lord. Amen.

(Adapted from the Roman liturgy)

* * *

Reflections

Pray in the Spirit at all times.

(Ephesians 6.18)

They who pray without ceasing unite all good in this one thing.

(Symeon the new theologian)

There are not two separate kingdoms, one for the living and one for the dead. There is only God's kingdom and, living or dead, we are all therein.

(Georges Bernanos)

I remembered the Lord

I remembered the Lord, and my prayer came to you in your holy temple. With a voice of thanksgiving I will sacrifice to you; what I have vowed, I will do. Deliverance belongs to the Lord.

(Adapted from Jonah 2)

Remember us, Lord

Hear us, Lord our God, and have pity on us, for you are merciful. May our steps hold to your paths, and may our feet not slip; guide us, Lord, in your way and we shall walk in your truth. May our prayer come before you, Lord; turn your ear to our cry, for our souls are full of trouble. Remember us, Lord, in your goodness and visit us with your salvation.

For you are the God of all mercy and full of compassion; yours is the glory, Father, Son and Holy Spirit, now and for ever, to the ages of ages. Amen.

(Orthodox)

Past, present and future

Eternal God and Father, help us to entrust the past to your mercy, the present to your love, and the future to your wisdom, in the name of Jesus Christ our Lord, who is the same yesterday, and today, and for ever. Amen.

(Anon)

Steer the ship of our life

Lord our God, teach us to ask you for those blessings of which we are most in need. Steer the ship of our life towards yourself, you who are the tranquil haven of all storm-tossed souls. Show us the course we should follow. Let your Spirit curb our wilfulness and guide and enable us in what is good, to keep your laws, and in all our works for ever to rejoice in your glorious and gladdening presence. For yours is the glory and praise from all your saints, for ever and ever. Amen.

(Adapted from Saint Basil)

For one who is dying

All-powerful and merciful Father, in the death of Christ you have opened a gateway to eternal life. Look kindly on (*name*) who is now close to death. United to the passion and death of your Son, and saved by the blood he shed, may (*name*) come before you with confidence; through the same Christ our Lord. Amen.

(Pope Paul VI)

Blessing

May almighty God strengthen our faith with proofs of his love, so that we may persevere in good works.
May he direct our steps to himself, and show us how to walk in charity and peace. Amen.

(Adapted from the Roman liturgy)

* * *

Reflections

Who do you say that I am?

(Mark 8.29)

The Eucharist is the primary sacrament of reconciliation. Going to the Eucharist is not a moral statement; we go to the Eucharist because we need health, not because we are healthy.

(Ronald Rolheiser)

We are all in the gutter, but some of us are looking at the stars.

(Oscar Wilde)

My heart and soul

Lord my God, give me the will to obey your commandments, to be faithful to you, and to serve you with all my heart and soul.

(Adapted from Joshua 22)

Keep us in faith

Lord, you have honoured us with your own image and given us free will; deliver us from all afflictions that oppress us; keep us in faith and justice all the days of our life, and let us do all things in accordance with your will.

For yours is the greatness, the majesty, the power and the glory, Father, Son and Holy Spirit, now and for ever, to the ages of ages. Amen.

(Orthodox)

Self-offering

Take and receive, Lord, all my liberty, my memory, my understanding and my will, all that I have and own.

You gave them to me; to you, Lord, I return them. They are all yours; do with them what you will. Give me your love and your grace; these are enough for me; then I am rich enough. I do not ask anything more. Amen.

(Ignatius Loyola)

The gift of your divine love

Lord Jesus Christ, you have said, 'Ask and you shall receive; seek and you shall find; knock and the door shall be opened to you'; grant us the gift of your divine love so that we may ever love you with our whole heart in all our words and works, and never cease praising you, who with the Father and the Holy Spirit live and reign, God, for ever and ever. Amen.

(Anon, from India)

Married love

Creator Spirit, we thank you for your gift of sexual love by which husband and wife express their delight in each other, find refreshment, and share with you the joy of creating new life. By your grace may (*name*) and (*name*) remain lovers, rejoicing in your goodness; through Christ our Lord. Amen.

(Anglican Church of Aotearoa/New Zealand)

God's loving care

Father, I thank you for your promise that nothing can come between us and the love of Christ, even if we are troubled or worried, ill or suffering; because I am certain that neither death nor life, nothing in the past, nothing here and now, nothing that is to come, can come between me and your love, Father, in Christ Jesus our Lord. Amen.

(Congregation of the Most Holy Redeemer, adapted from Romans 8.38–39)

* * *

Reflections

What a long way it is between knowing God and loving him.

(Blaise Pascal)

An isolated humanism is an inhuman humanism.

(Henri de Lubac)

As there is wedlock between a husband and wife, so there is wedlock between God and the soul.

(Meister Eckhart)

Hear our prayer, Lord

Hear our prayer, Lord: bless, protect and sanctify all those who bow their heads before you; through the grace, mercy and infinite love of your only-begotten Son, to whom with you and your most holy, gracious and life-giving Spirit be blessing, now and for ever. Amen.

(Orthodox)

Receive our evening prayers

Blessed are you, God, almighty Lord, who made the sun to give light to the day and brightened the night with shining stars: you have brought us through this long day and led us to the threshold of night; hear our prayer and the prayers of your people. Forgive us all the sins we have committed deliberately or in weakness. Receive our evening prayers and pour out upon your adopted children the riches of your goodness and mercy. Set your holy angels round about us, clothe us with justice, strengthen us with your truth and defend us with your power. Deliver us from every attack of the devil who seeks to ensnare us. Grant that this evening, and the night to come, and all the days of our life may pass in holiness and peace, without our falling into sin or error, through the mediation of the holy mother of God and all the saints who have found favour with you since time began.

For you indeed, Lord our God, have mercy on us and save us, and we glorify you, Father, Son and Holy Spirit, now and for ever. Amen.

(Orthodox)

Perfect trust

May almighty God, the source of every good and of every grace flowing ceaselessly into our souls, grant us to have perfect trust in Christ our Lord, and to win his mercy. May he teach us to think correctly, honestly and with purpose, so that our minds may always be truly alert to the voice of our Lord speaking in us.

(Adapted from the Benedictional of John Longlonde)

Unless you lead me

I cannot dance, Lord, unless you lead me. If you will that I leap joyfully then you must be the first to dance and to sing! Then, and only then, will I leap for love. Then will I soar from love to knowledge, from knowledge to fruition, from fruition to beyond all human sense. And there will I remain for evermore.

(Mechthild of Magdeburg)

Free your servants

Almighty God, you know our needs before we ask and our ignorance in asking; free your servants from all anxious thoughts about tomorrow. Give us contentment with your good gifts; and confirm our faith so that, according as we seek first your kingdom, you will not allow us to lack anything which is necessary; through Christ our Lord. Amen.

(Adapted from Saint Augustine)

Blessing

May God's grace be with all who love our Lord Jesus Christ with undying love. Amen.

(Adapted from Ephesians 6)

* * *

Reflections

What shall it profit a person to gain the whole world and suffer the loss of the soul?

(Adapted from Mark 8.36; Douai)

As we pray, so we believe.

('Lex orandi, lex credendi', attributed to Pope Celestine I)

If you wish to see God there in heaven or here on earth, your heart must first become a pure mirror.

(Angelus Silesius)

Instruct me, Lord

Instruct me, Lord, in your way; on an even path lead me.

(Psalm 26.11)

You alone know what we need

Lord, we do not know what we should ask of you, but you already know what we need. You love us better than we know how to love ourselves. Father, give to us, your children, that which we do not know how to ask. We have no desire other than to do your will. Teach us to pray. Pray in us; in Jesus' name. Amen.

(François de la Mothe Fénélon)

Help us to be ready to give

God our Father, we thank you for your Son Jesus Christ, the Saviour of all people. Help us to take every talent and gift which we possess and to lay them on the altar of your service, that we too may be used to bring others to you. Help us to be ready to give, and even to sacrifice, our time, our energy, our money, to spread Christ's message wherever we live and to share with others the life of Christ which is in us. Help us so to live that by our words and our lives many more may be moved to give their minds and hearts to you. God our Father, hear this prayer through our Saviour Jesus Christ. Amen.

(Adapted from Catholic Prayer Book, Zimbabwe)

Bring us to repentance

Look mercifully, Lord, on all who sin against you, and, in your great kindness, bring us to repentance, so that, rejecting what is evil we may walk before you in holiness of life; for the sake of Jesus Christ our mediator and advocate. Amen.

(Adapted from an Anglican source)

The Holy Family

Father, we look to your loving guidance and order as the pattern of all family life. By following the example of the holy family of your Son, in mutual love and respect, may we come to the joy of our home in heaven. We ask this through the same Christ our Lord. Amen.

(Adapted from the Roman liturgy)

Sincerity in speech

Do you, Lord, take care of us and guard us against making light of truth by careless talk. Let us remind ourselves of the sincerity of your own speech and then our words will be well-chosen, thereby saving us much trouble. Shield us with your protection from the false attraction of untruth, and so keep us in body and soul worthy of our high Christian dignity. Amen.

(Adapted from a Spanish Collect, seventh century)

* * *

Reflections

One who has the spirit of prayer will find time for actual prayer. Whoever does not find time for prayer does not have the spirit of prayer.

(Capuchin documents)

We are neither the masters, nor the authors, but the guardians, the heralds, and the ministers of the word of God.

(Pope Paul VI, Evangelii Nuntiandi)

Let the same mind be in you that was in Christ Jesus.

(Philippians 2.5)

Rejoice in freedom

Grant, Lord, we ask you, the gladness of home to those who are far away, and freedom to those who are unjustly imprisoned, so that your people may rejoice in the freedom which your mercy grants us, both in this world and in the world to come. Amen.

(Gothic Missal)

The same mind that was in Christ Jesus

Father of all, who gave your only-begotten Son to take upon himself the form of a servant and to be obedient even to death on a cross, give us the same mind that was in Christ Jesus so that, sharing his humility, we may come to be with him in his glory, who is alive and reigns with you and the Holy Spirit, one God, now and for ever. Amen.

(Society of Saint Francis)

All peoples and nations

Almighty and ever-living God, who has willed to restore all things in your well-beloved Son, the King and Lord of all, mercifully grant that all peoples and nations, though divided and wounded by sin, may accept his gentle and loving rule, he who lives and reigns with you and the Holy Spirit, one God, for ever and ever. Amen.

(Adapted from an Anglican source)

You alone are inexhaustible

You, my God, are ever new although you are the most ancient – you alone are the food for eternity. I am to live for ever, not for a time, and I have no power over my being; I cannot destroy myself even if I wished to do so. I must live on, with intellect and consciousness for ever, in spite of myself. Without you, eternity would be another name for eternal misery. In you alone I have what can support me for ever; you alone are the food of my soul. You alone are inexhaustible, and ever offer me something new to know, something new to love. And so on for eternity I shall ever be like a child being taught the rudiments of your infinite divine nature. For you are yourself the seat and centre of all good, and the only substance in this universe of shadows, and the heaven in which blessed spirits live and rejoice. Amen.

(Adapted from John Henry Newman)

Joy that will never end

Lord, guard the rock of our faith in your only Son who was born of the virgin Mother with a body like ours, and from all eternity shares your glory. Free your people from present distress, and give them the joy that will never end.

(Adapted from the Roman liturgy)

Blessing

Grace, mercy and peace will be with us from God the Father and from Jesus Christ, the Father's Son, in truth and love. Amen.

(2 John 3)

* * *

Reflections

Do you love me?

(John 21.15)

It is undoubtedly true that if we could see and know ourselves as we are, we would be truly humble.

(Adapted from The Cloud of Unknowing)

Love! – and say it with your life!

(Saint Augustine)

Joy in the Lord

Cry out with joy to the Lord, all the earth.
Serve the Lord with gladness. Come before him, singing
  for joy.
Know that he, the Lord, is God.
He made us, we belong to him; we are his people, the
  sheep of his flock.
Go within his gates, giving thanks.
Enter his courts with songs of praise. Give thanks to
  him and bless his name.
Indeed, how good is the Lord, eternal his merciful love.
He is faithful from age to age.

(Adapted from Psalm 100)

Life means Christ

For me, life means Christ, for my heart was made for you,
  and it is restless until it rests in you who are the source of
  all life, all love, all light.
In your mercy is my trust; in your compassion is my hope;
in your will is my peace; in your grace is my dignity;
in your salvation is my security; in your love is my happiness;
in you alone is my identity.
Teach me to die to self that I may live more fully to you, live
  a life in you, with you and for you.
Renew my inner self that I may love others as you love me.
Be exalted in me by using me in any way that glorifies you.

(Anon, adapted from Saint Augustine)

Courage to seek unity

Heavenly Father, who called us in the body of your Son Jesus
Christ to continue his work of reconciliation and reveal you to
all the world: forgive us the sins which tear us apart, give us the
courage to overcome our fears and to seek that gift of unity

which is your gift and your will; through Jesus Christ our Lord. Amen.

(*Society of Saint Francis*)

The world was created by your word

Lord God, how did you create heaven and earth? Certainly it was neither in heaven nor on the earth that you made them, nor in the air or water which are part of heaven and earth; nor could you create the universe from within the universe, since nowhere existed in which to do it before it had itself been created. You did not even hold in your hand something from which to extract heaven and earth, because where could you have taken it from if you had not already made it? Is there anything that exists other than because you exist? So you gave the word and the world was created; you created it by your word. Amen.

(*Adapted from Saint Augustine*)

* * *

Reflections

A person cannot live without joy. That is why it is necessary that someone deprived of spiritual joys goes over into bodily pleasures.

(*Saint Thomas Aquinas*)

Discussion is the beginning of every work, and counsel precedes every undertaking.

(*Sirach 37.16*)

Never say no from pride or yes from weakness.

(*Anon*)

Serve you always with a pure mind

Glorious and almighty God, in whom all the blessed place the confidence of their hope, grant to us, by their help, that we may be enabled to serve you always with a pure mind; through Christ our Lord. Amen.

(Sarum Breviary)

Have mercy on all who wish me harm

Almighty God, have mercy on (*name*), and on all who wish me harm. Have mercy on their faults and on mine together by such easy, tender, merciful means as your infinite wisdom can best devise. Bring us both to heaven together, where we may always live and love together with you and your blessed saints, glorious Trinity, for the sake of the bitter suffering of our Saviour, Jesus Christ. Amen.

(Thomas More)

Do not leave us to our sins

Almighty Lord God, your glory cannot be approached, your compassion knows no bounds, and your love for all mankind is beyond human expression. In your mercy look on us and on all your people; do not leave us to our sins, but deal with us according to your goodness. Guide us to the haven of your will, and make us truly obedient to your commandments, so that we may not feel ashamed when we come before your judgement seat.

For you, God, are good and ever-loving, and we glorify you, Father, Son, and Holy Spirit, now and for ever, to the ages of ages. Amen.

(Orthodox)

Persevere until death

My God, I am poor and weak. Enrich me with your grace and make me strong enough to conquer temptation. May I seek the things that please you, and turn away from anything that displeases you, so that I may persevere until death in doing your will. Amen.

(Anon, from India)

Trust in the Lord God for ever

Those of steadfast mind you keep in peace – in peace
  because they trust in you.
Trust in the Lord for ever, for in the Lord God you have
  an everlasting rock.
In the path of your judgements, Lord, we wait for you;
your name and your renown are the soul's desire.
My soul yearns for you in the night, my spirit within
  me earnestly seeks you.
Lord, you will ordain peace for us, for indeed, all that we
  have done, you have done for us.

(Adapted from Isaiah 26.3–4, 8–9, 12)

Blessing

May God make us worthy of his call and fulfil by his power every good resolve and work of faith, so that the name of our Lord Jesus may be glorified in us, and we in him, according to the grace of God and the Lord Jesus Christ.

(Adapted from 2 Thessalonians 1.11–12)

* * *

Reflections

The sooner we get disillusioned with the church the better, because then we will learn that the church lives by the grace of God.

(Dietrich Bonhoeffer)

Give up your self and you will find your real self.

(C. S. Lewis)

Judgement will be without mercy to anyone who has shown no mercy; mercy triumphs over judgement.

(James 2.13)

Acts of faith, hope and charity

Lord Jesus, I accept all that you teach and the way of life you point out to me because your word is true. I believe; Lord, help my unbelief.

Lord Jesus, I have complete confidence in your promise calling me to eternal life. Give me all the help I need to remain true to you. Sacred Heart of Jesus, I place all my trust in you.

Lord Jesus, fill my heart with the Spirit of your love so that I may love you with all my heart and share that love with others.

(Anon)

Let me live for you

Rule all by your wisdom Lord, so that I may always serve you according to your will, and not as I choose. Do not punish me, I ask you, by granting what I wish or ask, if it offends your love, because I want your love to live always in my soul. Let me deny myself so that I may serve you. Let me live for you who in yourself are the true life. Amen.

(Teresa of Avila)

I place my soul in your hands

My Father, I abandon myself to you. Do with me as you will. Whatever you may do with me, I thank you. I am prepared for anything, I accept everything. Provided your will is fulfilled in me and in all creatures, I ask for nothing more, my God. I place my soul in your hands. I give it to you, my God, with all the love of my heart because I love you. For me, this gift of myself, this placing of myself in your hands without reserve in boundless confidence is a necessity of love, because you are my Father.

(Charles de Foucauld)

Your image in my family

Lord Jesus, with Mary and Joseph, you lived in a family; teach me to appreciate the gift of being part of a family. Show me ever new ways of protecting and comforting those closest to me; and, each day, let me do something that will say 'I love you' without speaking those words. Let me never part from any of my family in anger; prompt me always to turn back without delay to forgive and to be forgiven. Let me see your image in my family, in each of them, and in my larger family too, knowing that, in your kingdom, we will be truly one family, united by your sacrifice on the cross. Amen.

(Anon)

On the cross, Lord Jesus Christ

On the cross, Lord Jesus Christ, you stretched out your hands for the salvation of the human race. Grant that our life and work may be pleasing to you and bear witness to the power of your redeeming love; you who live and reign for ever and ever. Amen.

(Adapted from the Roman liturgy)

* * *

Reflections

On the road to union with God, the night of faith shall guide me.

(John of the Cross)

Father . . . not my will, but yours, be done.

(Luke 22.42)

There are many whom God has and the church does not have. And there are many whom the church has, and God does not have them.

(Saint Augustine)

My soul is thirsting for you, my God

Like the deer that yearns for running streams,
so my soul is thirsting for you, my God.
My soul is thirsting for God, the God of my life;
when can I enter and see the face of God?
My tears have become my bread, by night, by day,
as I hear it said all the day long: 'Where is your God?'
These things will I remember as I pour out my soul:
how I would lead the rejoicing crowd into the house of God,
amid cries of gladness and thanksgiving, the throng wild
    with joy.
Why are you cast down, my soul, why groan within me?
Hope in God; I will praise him still, my Saviour and my God.
Deep is calling on deep in the roar of waters;
your torrents and all your waves swept over me.
By day the Lord will send his loving-kindness;
by night I will sing to him, praise the God of my life.
I will say to God, my rock: 'Why have you forgotten me?
Why do I go mourning, oppressed by the foe?'
With cries that pierce me to the heart, my enemies revile me,
saying to me all the day long: 'Where is your God?'
Why are you cast down, my soul, why groan within me?
Hope in God; I will praise him still, my Saviour and my God.

(Adapted from Psalm 42)

Blessing

May our Lord Jesus Christ himself and God our Father, who
loved us and through grace gave us eternal comfort and good
hope, comfort our hearts and strengthen them in every good
work and word. Amen.

(Adapted from 2 Thessalonians 2.16–17)

* * *

Reflections

Stand up and raise your heads, because your redemption is drawing near.

(Luke 21.28)

Our best chance of finding God is where we left him.

(Meister Eckhart)

In every person there is a part that is afraid of healing, that does not want change – a brokenness with which one has learned to live, and which seems safer than the unknown.

(Jean Vanier)

A blessing on children

Blest are you, my God, with every pure blessing;
let all your chosen ones bless you.
Let them bless you for ever.
Blest are you because you have made me glad.
You have dealt with us according to your great mercy.
Blest are you because you had compassion on my children.
Be merciful to them, Master, and keep them safe;
bring their lives to fulfilment in happiness and mercy.

(Adapted from Tobit 8.15–17)

A prayer for relatives and friends

Have mercy, Lord, on all those who are our relatives and
friends, and grant that they, with us, may be so conformed to
your will, that being cleansed from all sin, we may be found
worthy, by the inspiration of your love, to partake together in
the blessedness of your heavenly kingdom; through Jesus Christ
our Lord. Amen.

(Adapted from the Gallican Sacramentary)

As age advances

Almighty God, by your mercy I have reached my present age;
grant that this mercy may not be in vain. Do not let my years be
multiplied so as to increase my guilt, but, as age advances, let
me become more pure in my thoughts, more regular in my
desires, and more obedient to your laws. Do not let the cares of
the world distract me, nor the evils of age overwhelm me, but
continue to increase your loving-kindness towards me, and,
when you shall call me, receive me to everlasting happiness, for
the sake of Jesus Christ our Lord. Amen.

(Adapted from Samuel Johnson)

Hail, holy Lady

Hail, holy Lady, most holy queen, Mary, mother of God, ever virgin; chosen by the most holy Father in heaven, consecrated by him, with his most beloved Son and the Holy Spirit, the Comforter. On you descended and in you still remains all the fullness of grace. Hail, his palace! Hail, his tabernacle! Hail, his robe! Hail, his handmaid! Hail, his mother! And hail, all holy virtues, who, by the grace and inspiration of the Holy Spirit, are poured into the hearts of the faithful so that, faithless no longer, they may be made faithful servants of God through you. Amen.

(Adapted from Saint Francis of Assisi)

Grant us your peace

Holy Father, keep us in your truth;
Holy Son, protect us under your cross;
Holy Spirit, make us temples and dwelling-places
   for your glory;
grant us your peace all the days of our lives, Lord. Amen.

(Maronite Church)

* * *

Reflections

The people who get things done . . . are those who do one thing at a time.

(Kallistos Ware)

Whoever does not provide for relatives, and especially for family members, has denied the faith and is worse than an unbeliever.

(1 Timothy 5.8)

In the end, life offers only one tragedy: not to have been a saint.

(Charles Péguy)

Preparing for Communion

Lord Jesus Christ our God, have mercy on us. Amen.

Heavenly King, Comforter, Spirit of truth, who are
  everywhere and fill all things, the treasure of blessings
  and giver of life, come and abide in us. Clean us of all
  impurity, and, in your goodness, save us.

Holy God, holy and mighty, holy and immortal, have mercy
  on us.

Glory be to the Father, and to the Son, and to the
  Holy Spirit, as it was in the beginning, is now, and
  ever shall be, world without end. Amen.

Most holy Trinity, have mercy on us. Lord, clean us of our
  sins. Master, pardon our faults. Holy One, visit us and
  heal our weaknesses for your name's sake.

Lord, have mercy. Christ, have mercy. Lord, have mercy.

Come, let us worship God our King.

Come, let us worship before Christ, our King and our God.

Come, let us worship and fall down before Christ himself,
  our King and our God. Amen.

(Orthodox)

The food of your word

God, you have taught us that we do not live on bread alone but
by every word that comes from the mouth of God. Grant us
always to hunger for the food of your word, which you have
given for our nourishment to eternal life; through Christ our
Lord. Amen.

(Adapted from an Anglican source)

For those who travel

Heavenly Father, protector of those who trust in you, you led
your people in safety through the desert, and brought them to
a land of plenty. Guide your faithful people (*names*) who are
travelling today. Fill them with your spirit of love. Preserve them

from all harm, and bring them in safety to their destination. We ask this through Christ our Lord. Amen.

(Adapted from the Roman liturgy)

For the aged

Eternal Father, you who are unchanged down the changing years, be near to those who are aged. Even though their bodies weaken, grant that their spirit may be strong; may they bear weakness and affliction with patience, and, at the end, meet death with serenity; through Christ our Lord. Amen.

(Pope Paul VI)

Commendation

May Mary's prayers win us a peaceful night and a welcome home at the end of our pilgrimage on earth. Amen.

(Anon)

* * *

Reflections

Do you also wish to go away?

(John 6.67)

Does your mind desire the strength to gain mastery over your passions? Let it submit to a greater power, and it will conquer all beneath it. And peace will be in you – true, sure, ordered peace. What is that order? God as ruler of the mind; the mind as ruler of the body. Nothing could be more orderly.

(Saint Augustine)

The real challenge is not to discover new lands but to see the present land with new eyes.

(Adapted from Marcel Proust)

REFERENCES AND ACKNOWLEDGEMENTS

Every effort has been made to trace the owners of copyright material, and we hope that no copyright has been infringed. Pardon is sought and apology made if the contrary be the case, and a correction will be made in any reprint of this book.

The following is a list of the principal sources consulted in the preparation of this book:

Appleton, George (ed.), *The Oxford Book of Prayer*, Oxford University Press, Oxford, 1985.

Armstrong, Regis and Brady, Ignatius, *Praying with Saint Francis of Assisi*, Triangle, London, 1987.

Barclay, William, *Prayers for Young People* and *More Prayers for Young People*, St Pauls/BYB, Mumbai, India (no year). Used with permission.

Bedard, Vicki Wells and Rabior, William, *Prayers for Catholics Experiencing Divorce*, Liguori Publications, Liguori, Montana, 1993.

Blácam, Aodh de, *Gaelic Literature Surveyed: From Earliest Times to the Present*, Talbot Press, Dublin, 1973.

Bloom, Metropolitan Anthony, *Living Prayer* and *School for Prayer*, DLT, London, 1975.

Boldoni, Valeria (comp.), *Praying with Augustine*, trans. Paula Clifford, Triangle, London, 1997.

Bullen, Anthony and Brandley, James A., *Catholic Prayer Book*, Gweru, Zimbabwe, 1971.

Carmichael, Alexander (comp.), *Carmina Gadelica: Hymns and Incantations with Illustrative Notes and Words, Rites and Customs, Dying and Obsolete*, Scottish Academic Press, Edinburgh, six vols, from 1900. Used with permission.

Catholic Truth Society, London, for extracts from papal encyclicals and church documents. Also for Dessain, Charles Stephen, *The Mind of Cardinal Newman*, 1974; Le Morvan, Michael, *Pierre Teilhard de Chardin, Priest and Evolutionist*, 1979; Anon, *A Hospital Prayer Book*, no date; Anon, *A Simple Penance Book*, 1998.

Caussade, Jean-Pierre de, *The Sacrament of the Present Moment*, trans.

Kitty Muggeridge, Fount, London, 1981.

Chapman, Dom John, *Spiritual Letters*, Sheed and Ward, London, 1935.

Clare, Mother Mary, *The Simplicity of Prayer*, SLG Press, Fairacres, Oxford, 1988. Copyright The Sisters of the Love of God.

CTS/SPCK, *The Anglican-Roman Catholic International Commission: The Final Report*, London, 1981.

Every, George, Harries, Richard and Ware, Kallistos (eds), *Seasons of the Spirit: Readings through the Christian Year*, Triangle, London, 1990.

Flannery, Austin (ed.), *Vatican Council II: The Conciliar and Post-Conciliar Documents*, two vols, Costello Publishing Company, USA, 1975. Used with permission.

Fox, Selina Fitzherbert, *A Chain of Prayer Across the Ages: Forty Centuries of Prayer 2000 BC–2000 AD*, John Murray, London, 1941. Used with permission.

French, R. M. (ed.), *The Way of a Pilgrim* and *The Pilgrim Continues His Way*, Triangle, London, 1995.

Fromm, Erich, *The Art of Loving*, Unwin, London, 1971.

Gibbard, Mark, *Twentieth-Century Men of Prayer*, SCM Press, London, 1974. Used with permission.

Grant, Paul (ed.), *A Dazzling Darkness: An Anthology of Western Mysticism*, Collins, London, 1985.

The Holy Bible, New Revised Standard Version, Catholic edition, London, 1993. The Scripture quotations contained herein are from the New Revised Standard Version Bible: Catholic Edition copyright 1989 by the Division of Christian Education of the National Council of the Churches of Christ in the USA. Used by permission. All rights reserved.

Hurley, Dermot, *Everyday Prayerbook*, Chapman, London, 1979.

John Paul II, Pope, *Crossing the Threshold of Hope*, ed. Vittorio Messori, Jonathan Cape, London, 1994.

Johnston, William, *Silent Music* and *The Wounded Stag*, published in one volume as *The Mystical Way*, Fount, London, 1993.

Keane, Frank, *Blessed Edmund Rice 1762–1844*, Waterford, Ireland, 1996.

Kreeft, Peter (ed.), *Christianity for Modern Pagans: Pascal's Pensées*, Ignatius Press, San Francisco, 1993.

Law, Philip (comp.), *Praying with the Old Testament* and *Praying with*

the New Testament, Triangle, London, 1989.
Lawrence of the Resurrection, Brother, *An Oratory of the Heart* (ed. Robert Llewellyn), St. Paul Publications, Bombay, 1984. Used with permission.

Main, John, *Word Into Silence, Moment of Christ* and *The Present Christ*, published in one volume as *The Inner Christ*, DLT, London, 1994.
McEvoy, Hubert (ed.), *Priestly Prayers*, Burns, Oates and Washbourne, London, 1961. By permission of Burns & Oates.

Neuner, J. and Dupuis, J. (eds), *The Christian Faith in the Doctrinal Documents of the Catholic Church*, Collins, London, 1983.

Obbard ODC, Elizabeth Ruth, *A Retreat with Thérèse of Lisieux: Loving Our Way Into Holiness*, Saint Anthony Messenger Press, Cincinnati, Ohio, copyright 1996. Reprinted by permission of St Anthony Messenger Press, 1615 Republic St., Cincinnati, OH 45210, USA. All rights reserved.
O'Collins, Gerald, *Experiencing Jesus*, SPCK, London, 1994.
Ó Laoghaire, Diarmuid (ed.), *Our Mass, Our Life: Some Irish Traditions and Prayers*, Messenger Publications, Dublin, 1968. Used with permission.
Ó Riordáin, John J. (ed.), *Lifelines*, no place, 1990.

Parenti, Stefano (ed.), *Praying with the Orthodox Tradition*, trans. Paula Clifford, Triangle, London, 1989.
Paulines, The, *The Catechism of the Catholic Church*, Mambo Press, Zimbabwe, 1994.
Perry, Whitall N., *A Treasury of Traditional Wisdom*, George Allen and Unwin, London, 1971.
Powell, John, *Unconditional Love*, Tabor Publishing, Allen, Texas, 1978, and *Why Am I Afraid to Love?* Fount, London, 1991.

Redemptorists, The Irish, *Come, Lord Jesus: Redemptorist Mission and Novena Book*, Dublin, no date. Used with permission.
Rieu, E. V., *Early Christian Writings*, Penguin Classics, London, 1978.
Robinson, Wendy, *Exploring Silence*, SLG Press, Fairacres, Oxford, 1995.
Rolheiser, Ronald, *Against an Infinite Horizon*, Hodder & Stoughton, London, 1995. Used with permission.
Rotelle, John E. (ed.), *Augustine Day by Day: Minute Meditations Taken from the Writings of Saint Augustine*, Catholic Book Publishing Co., New York, 1986; and *Tradition Day by Day: Readings from Church Writers*, Augustinian Press, Villanova, Pennsylvania, 1994.

Saint Vladimir's Seminary Press, *A Manual of Eastern Orthodox Prayers*, Crestwood, New York, 1983.

Shaw, Gilbert, *A Pilgrim's Book of Prayers*, SLG Press, Fairacres, Oxford, 1992.

Simpson, Ray (comp.), *Celtic Daily Light: A Spiritual Journey Throughout the Year*, Hodder & Stoughton, London, 1997. Used with permission.

Society of Saint Francis, *Celebrating Common Prayer*, Mowbray, London, 1997. Used with permission.

SPCK, *The SPCK Book of Christian Prayer*, Society for Promoting Christian Knowledge, London, 1996.

Staniforth, Maxwell, *Early Christian Writings*, Penguin Classics, London, 1968. Copyright Maxwell Staniforth.

The Tablet: The International Catholic Weekly, London, for occasional extracts from articles by various authors, or from *The Living Spirit* column.

Tugwell, Simon, *Prayer*, two vols, Veritas, Dublin, 1974.

Vanier, Jean, *The Broken Body: Journey to Wholeness*, St. Pauls/BYB, Mumbai, India, 1993. Used with permission.

Vatican Polyglot Press, *The Pope's Family Prayer Book*, Vatican City, 1975.

Voillaume, René, *Seeds of the Desert: The Legacy of Charles de Foucauld*, Anthony Clarke Books, 1973.

Ward, Benedicta, *The Wisdom of the Desert Fathers*, SLG Press, Fairacres, Oxford, 1995.

Ware, Bishop Kallistos, *The Power of the Name: The Jesus Prayer in Orthodox Spirituality*, SLG Press, Fairacres, Oxford, 1991.

Watts, Murray (comp.), *The Wisdom of Saint Columba of Iona*, Past Times, Oxford, 1997.

Weyer, Robert van de (ed.), *Celtic Fire: An Anthology of Celtic Christian Literature*, DLT, London, 1990.

GLOSSARY OF AUTHORS AND TERMS

(In some cases, little or no information is available about contributors; therefore they are omitted. This is especially true of contemporary writers about whom there is no information in sources such as encyclopaedias or dictionaries of biography. See pages 114–117 for references to authors' works.

Alberione, Venerable James (1894–1971) Born in the Piedmont region of northern Italy. At the age of sixteen, James Alberione received a special call from God on the night between the nineteenth and twentieth centuries, which compelled him to do something for the people of the century just beginning. He became a priest and founded the Pauline Family of men and women religious, who communicate the Gospel of Jesus Christ through the media. John Paul II has called him 'the first apostle of the new evangelization'.

Alcuin (735–804) Flaccus Albinus Alcuinus was born in York, England, where he became head of the cathedral school and established a library. In 782 Charlemagne called him to Aix-la-Chapelle to organize a school in the palace. In 796 he retired to the abbey of Saint Martin of Tours and founded a school there also. His writings include works on grammar, rhetoric, dialectic, astronomy, dogma, poetry, a revision of the Vulgate and a Missal. He is regarded as the virtual founder of education in the Frankish empire and the inspiration of the Carolingian renaissance.

Alphonsus Liguori, Saint (1696–1787) Born in Naples, Italy, he became a lawyer, then a priest in 1726. He founded the Redemptoristine nuns, and the Congregation of the Most Holy Redeemer (the Redemptorists) to preach the Christian faith to the people. His own speciality was moral theology where his outlook was gentle and liberal. In later life his relations with his own congregation were strained and he was removed from its leadership by Pope Pius VI. He was later made bishop and cardinal.

Ambrose of Milan, Saint (340–97) Born in Trier, Germany. Trained in law, he entered the civil service of the Roman empire, becoming a provincial governor, residing in Milan. He was chosen by popular acclaim as the city's bishop, even though he was still unbaptized. After baptism and ordination, he gave his property to the poor and began an intensive study of Scripture. He strongly opposed Arianism, a heresy which questioned the divinity of Christ. He had many conflicts with the Emperor Theodosius, insisting that a Christian emperor had to live like a Christian. He helped Saint Augustine in his difficulties with the Christian faith, and later baptized him. His feast is celebrated on 7 December.

Ambrosiaster (mid to late fourth century) The name coined by Erasmus for the unknown author of a commentary on the letters of Saint Paul previously thought to have been written by Saint Ambrose. Erasmus concluded, on the basis of internal textual evidence, that it could not have been written by Ambrose. In 1905, studies showed that a collection of some 127 Questions on the Old and New Testaments until then attributed to Saint Augustine were the work of the same person. Nothing is known of him except that he lived in Rome, knew Roman law, wrote Latin well and had an interest in things Jewish, but was not himself a Jew.

Angelus Silesius (1624–77) The pseudonym of Johannes Scheffler, a bishop and poet, born in Silesia. Influenced by theosophy, some of his writings have been translated into English.

Anselm of Canterbury, Saint (1033–1109) Born in Aosta, Italy, he joined the Benedictines in France, becoming abbot at Le Bec before going to England where he was chosen to be Archbishop of Canterbury. He struggled for the freedom of the church from royal control and was twice exiled. He also opposed the slave-trade. He wrote extensively on mystical theology of which his best-known work is on the incarnation, *Cur Deus Homo?* His feast is on 21 April.

Apostles' Creed A statement of the essential articles of the Christian faith dating from a baptismal catechesis of the second or third century, it has no known connection with the apostles, and is so called because it is divided into twelve sections.

Appleton, George Began work as a curate of the Church of England in the East End of London, then went as a missionary to Burma. After the Second World War, he returned to London, working at Saint Paul's Cathedral. He became archbishop of Perth in 1963, and archbishop in Jerusalem in 1969, retiring in 1974. He has published several books on prayer and spirituality.

Aristotle (384–322 BC) Born at Stagira, in Thrace, Greece, he was a pupil of Plato's for almost 20 years. He spent some time at the courts of King Philip of Macedon and of Alexander. He began his own school, the Peripatetic, in Athens about 335. He was the first to treat logic as a science and to give philosophy a systematic foundation, emphasizing the reality of things outside human consciousness. He has left a substantial body of writings.

Athanasius, Saint (297–373) Born in Alexandria, Egypt, the greater part of his life was taken up with the struggle against Arianism, which he first challenged publicly at the Council of Nicaea in 325. Becoming Bishop of Alexandria in 328, he was the great champion of the divinity of Christ, and he suffered much for this, being sent into exile on five different occasions, for a total of 17 years. Among his best-known writings is the treatise *On the Incarnation*. He is almost certainly not the author of the Athanasian Creed. His feast is celebrated on 2 May.

Augustine of Hippo, Saint (354–430) Born at Thagaste in Tunisia, of a Christian mother, Monica, and a pagan father, Patricius, his early life was marked by his adherence to Manicheism and his sexual promiscuity. He was converted to the Christian faith at about the age of 32, and was baptized by Saint Ambrose of Milan in 387. He described this spiritual journey in *The Confessions*, perhaps the first autobiography ever written. Returning to Africa, he founded a semi-monastic community, but, before long, he was chosen by popular acclamation and against his will to be bishop in the diocese of Hippo. Among his vast writings, one of the best-known is *On the City of God*, the first Christian philosophy of history, written to refute the charge that it was the conversion of Rome to Christianity which was bringing about its defeat by the barbarian tribes. Augustine died while Hippo was being besieged by the Vandals. His feast is celebrated on 28 August, the day after his mother, Saint Monica.

Barclay, William (1907–78) Ordained a minister in the Church of Scotland, he was for many years professor of Divinity and Biblical Criticism at the University of Glasgow. He wrote a commentary on the New Testament, and many other works, both popular and academic, in which he sought to bridge the gap between the academic world of theology and that of the plain person in the pew.

Basil, Saint (330–79) Born in Caesarea, Cappadocia, Turkey, he received an exceptional education. Though he would have preferred a quiet, retiring life he became Bishop of Caesarea in 370. He was noted for his efforts against Arianism, his concern for the poor, and for rehabilitating thieves and prostitutes. His writings are still widely read, especially those on the Holy Spirit and for monks, which are still followed by the Order of Saint Basil in the eastern church. His feast is celebrated annually on 2 January.

Benedict of Norcia, Saint (480–547) Born in Umbria, Italy, he studied in Rome before going to Subiaco to live a life of solitude. He later moved to Monte Cassino where he founded a monastery and wrote a rule of life for his followers, drawing on the writings of Saint Basil and Cassian, as well as his own good sense and moderation. The *Rule* recommended prayer, Scripture reading and manual work. Though never a priest his influence was very great, so that he is commonly regarded as the father of western monasticism. He was declared patron of Europe by Pope John Paul II. His feast is kept on 11 July.

Benedictional A benedictional is a book of blessings, or, more recently, one which contains the rite of Benediction of the Blessed Sacrament. The name derives from the Latin, *benedictio*, meaning a blessing.

Benson, Edward White (1829–96) An Englishman, he was ordained in the Anglican church, and was Archbishop of Canterbury from 1883 until his death.

Bernanos, Georges (1888–1948) A French writer, his *Diary of a Country Priest*, published in 1936, contains many spiritual insights.

Bernard of Clairvaux, Saint (1090–1153) Born near Dijon, France, he joined the Cistercians in 1111, bringing 30 companions with him, including four of his brothers. Soon after, he was elected abbot of Clairvaux, from which he founded 68 other monasteries. He preached in France and Germany in support of the second crusade against the Moslems, and another against the Albigensians, and was active in civil and church politics. He was an adviser to popes, especially Eugene III, one of his former monks; he participated in regional and ecumenical councils, wrote widely on theology and spirituality, and was involved in controversy with Abélard. Sometimes known as the last of the Fathers of the church, his feast is celebrated on 20 August.

Bloom, Anthony (1914–) Born in Lausanne, Switzerland, of Russian parents, he moved to Paris as a child. He qualified as a medical doctor and served in the French army during the Second World War. Converted from atheism, in 1948 he became a Russian Orthodox priest in Paris, and since 1966 has been Metropolitan of Sourozh. His writings include *Living Prayer, School for Prayer, God and Man* and *Meditations on a Theme.*

Bonhoeffer, Dietrich (1906–45) A German Lutheran theologian, active in the 'Confessing' church which opposed Nazism, he was executed for his part in the July 1944 plot against Hitler. His *Letters and Papers from Prison*, published in 1953, became a seminal source of radical theology, proposing a 'religionless' Christianity. He also wrote *The Cost of Discipleship.*

Breviary A book, or books, containing the Divine Office, said daily by priests, religious and some laypeople. It is based on the Psalms and other Scripture readings, with hymns and prayers.

Calvin, John (1509–64) Born at Noyon, France, he studied theology and law before becoming a preacher. In 1536 he went to Geneva to help the cause of the Reform there but was driven out as his ideas were considered extreme. Returning in 1541, he set up a system of church rule, despite much opposition. He had the Spanish Protestant theologian Servetus burned as a heretic. He wrote commentaries on many books of the Bible and the *Institutes of the Christian Religion*, and supported the Protestant cause in France and England.

Capuchin Order A branch of the Franciscan first order, it began as a reform movement by Fra Matteo da Bascio, and received papal approval in 1528. Its members follow the Rule of Saint Francis and their proper Constitutions. It now numbers some 11,000 friars in over 90 countries.

Carew, Andrew (1902–87) A priest of the Irish province of the Capuchin Franciscan friars.

Celtic spirituality Celtic spirituality began in the pre-Christian era, emphasizing a lack of distinction between the sacred and the secular, nature and grace, and thus seeing all of life, even routine daily events and activities, as invested with religious significance. There is a profound sense of the immanence, or all-pervading presence, of God in life. John Scotus Eriugena was the great theologian of the Celtic world. His theology was inclusive, and it took creation rather than redemption as its starting point. In God, creating and being are one, so that the created world is itself a theophany, or manifestation of God. But Celtic spirituality is also transcendent with a sense of the majesty and wonder of

God who is greater by far than his creatures. It is a gutsy, down-to-earth, vigorous spirituality which is at home with the world and with sexuality.

In the Christian world, the term 'Celtic' refers to Ireland, Scotland, Wales, the Isle of Man, Cornwall and Brittany, together with those parts of France, Germany, Switzerland and Italy where Saint Columbanus and his disciples founded monasteries. The Christian community adopted many of the ideas, attitudes and assumptions of pre-Christian Celtic tradition while seeking to remove elements which were incompatible with the Christian faith. The *Stowe Missal* and the *Carmina Gadelica* (six vols, Edinburgh, 1928) are outstanding examples of early and recent Celtic liturgy and spirituality.

Cerne, Book of A manuscript collection of prayers for private use, attributed to Aedelwald, a ninth-century Saxon bishop attached to the Benedictine monastery of Cerne, Dorset, England. Now in the university library, Cambridge.

Chapman, John A Benedictine monk who lived at the start of the twentieth century, and served as a chaplain to the British army during the First World War. He corresponded widely on spiritual matters, and some of this correspondence has been published under the title *Spiritual Letters*.

Chardin, Pierre Teilhard de (1881–1955) Born at Sarcenet, in the Auvergne, France, he entered the Jesuits and trained in England. A palaeontologist by profession, he sought to present Christ as the focal point to which all creation leads. Influential among scientists, he was prohibited by the Holy Office from teaching or publishing any religious writings due to their uncertain nature, but recently his works have enjoyed a renewed interest. He died in virtual exile in the United States. His writings such as *Le Milieu Divin*, *The Phenomenon of Man*, *Letters from a Traveller*, *Hymn of the Universe*, *The Future of Man* and *The Heart of Matter*, all published posthumously, have been widely influential.

Christarakana The Book of Common Prayer of the Anglican Church of India, Pakistan, Myanmar and Sri Lanka.

Clare of Assisi, Saint (1193–1253) Clare Offreducia was born in Assisi, Italy. On growing up, she followed the example of Francis of Assisi in living a life of intense devotion to God. She founded the contemplative nuns now known as the Poor Clares. A strong personality, she offered counsel to Saint Francis on the life of his brothers, and to many others including Pope Gregory IX. With her sisters, she cared for the sick while living a life of simplicity and poverty. Her feast is kept on 11 August.

Clement of Alexandria, Saint Titus Flavius Clemens was probably born in Athens, Greece, in the second century and brought up a pagan. Converted to Christianity, he spent most of his life in Alexandria, Egypt, though it seems that he left it permanently in about 202 during the persecution of the Roman emperor, Septimius Severus. A cultured Greek philosopher and scholar, a Christian apologist and exegete, Clement may not have been a priest but his concerns were pastoral and catechetical, combining the Christian faith and elements of Greek philosophy.

Cloud of Unknowing, The An anonymous work much influenced by the ideas of the pseudo-Dionysius, written in England in the latter half of the fourteenth century. Its central thesis is that the supreme knowledge of God is to recognize that we know nothing about him; he is hidden in a 'cloud' of unknowability. It is only by emptying the mind of all images and ideas of God, and the will of all earthly desires, that we can be drawn to union with God.

Collect The opening prayer of the Mass, which 'collects' into one the prayers of the congregation.

Columbanus, Saint (*c.* 543–615) Born in Leinster, Ireland, he studied the humanities before entering monastic life and travelling to France where he founded a number of monasteries. He was a firm defender of the rights and traditions of the Celtic church. Exiled to Italy, he founded a monastery at Bobbio. His extant writings, mainly his monastic *Rule*, poetry, letters, sermons and a treatise against the Arians, were republished under the editorship of G. S. M. Walker in 1970. His feast is celebrated on 23 November.

Common Prayer, Book of The official liturgical text for churches of the Anglican communion, it comprises in one volume a calendar, a lectionary, the rites of the Eucharist and the sacraments, the order of funerals, a profession of faith, and all rites needed for Anglican worship. The chief compiler was Thomas Cranmer, Archbishop of Canterbury, who drew on the Sarum Missal, the medieval breviary, ritual and pontifical as well as elements from the Gallican and Greek liturgies. Its classical literary excellence has influenced not only Anglican worship but the development of the English language. The best-known editions are those of 1662 and 1928, though each self-governing church of the Anglican communion is free to devise its own text. It has been translated into about 150 languages.

Coptic The word derives from the Greek, *Guptios*, meaning an Egyptian. The Coptic Church is found in Egypt and Ethiopia, dating from the fifth century. In its doctrine of Christ it holds to one nature rather than two, and it is nationalistic in outlook.

Cyprian of Carthage, Saint (*c.* 200–58) Having trained in law, he became a Christian in middle age, and Bishop of Carthage, Algeria, in 249. His writings were particularly concerned with unity in the church and with an attitude of tolerance to Christians who had apostatized from the faith in times of persecution. He was active in organizing help for sufferers during a plague in 252–54. During the persecution by the Emperor Valerian, he was first exiled and then beheaded. His feast is kept on 16 September.

Cyril of Jerusalem, Saint (315–86) He became Bishop of Jerusalem in 348. His involvement in the Arian controversy led to his being sent into exile three times for a total of 16 years. His extant writings are mainly in the form of catechesis for catechumens and the newly baptized. He was declared a doctor of the church in 1888; his feast is celebrated on 18 March.

Denis, Saint It is said that Denis went from Rome to France as a missionary in the middle of the third century, and that he became the first bishop of Paris. Little is known of him with certainty though he is said to have been beheaded about 258 on Montmartre, the hill of martyrs, by the Roman authorities with two of his priests during the persecution of the Emperor Valerian. His feast is celebrated on 9 October.

Dostoevsky, Fyodor (1821–81) Born in Moscow, Russia, the son of a doctor, he served for a time in the army. His writings, considered to be radical and socialist, caused him to fall foul of the tsarist authorities, who sentenced him to death. Reprieved, he served four years in a penal camp which had the effect of accentuating his epilepsy. His novels show profound spiritual and psychological insight., especially the discourses of Father Zossima in *The Brothers Karamazov*.

Douai The name of the town in Belgium where recusant English Catholics studied for the priesthood in the Elizabethan and post-Elizabethan period. A translation of the Bible into English from the Vulgate was done there and given that name. It was commonly in use among Catholics until the publication of the Jerusalem Bible in 1966.

Eckhart, Meister Johann (*c.* 1260–1327) Born at Hochheim in Germany, he joined the Dominican Order. A preacher, theologian and mystic, he used new language – for example, speaking of God as female

– in his theological writings. This involved him in difficulties with church leaders, even though his personal orthodoxy and morals were vindicated on examination. He taught theology in France and Germany and became the provincial of his Order in Saxony. He is regarded as the father of German mysticism.

Epistle to Diognetus An anonymously written apologetic in the form of a letter, from about the middle of the second century. Its theology is described as sincere but vague, its style noble and elegant. Nothing is known of its origins, or of Diognetus.

Etchells, Ruth is a distinguished lay theologian. Her books include *Unafraid to Be* and *Just As I Am*.

Fénélon, François de Salignac de la Mothe (1651–1715) Born in Périgord, France, he was an educationalist, theologian and Archbishop of Cambrai. A zealous pastor and vigorous controversialist, some of his writings in support of Mme Guyon, a prominent, if eccentric, contemporary spiritual writer, were condemned by Rome as being favourable to quietism. In economic affairs he favoured free trade, reduced government spending and a balanced budget and, in politics, a constitutional monarchy, parliamentary government, separation of church and state, and decentralization. It has been said that if his ideas had been implemented the French Revolution might never have occurred.

Foucauld, Charles de (1858–1916) Born in Strasbourg, France, he lost his faith while at secondary school. Joining the French army, he served in North Africa, but official disapproval of his excessive profligacy led to his abandoning a military career. In 1886 he experienced a profound religious conversion, following which he went to the Holy Land and Syria for some years. He spent seven years with the Cistercians, before leaving to become a hermit and priest in North Africa, where he produced the first dictionary in the Tuareg language. He is recognized as the founder of the Little Brothers and the Little Sisters of the Poor, religious congregations working among the poor. He was killed by a member of the Senussi sect.

Francis de Sales, Saint (1567–1623) Born at Annecy, France, he studied law in Paris, then was ordained priest and became Bishop of Geneva, Switzerland, in 1602. He worked hard for the education of clergy and faithful alike, insisting that the fullness of the Christian life was accessible to all. His two principal writings are *A Treatise on the Love of God* and *An Introduction to the Devout Life*, of which the latter was unique in its time in that it was written with laypeople particularly in mind. A renowned preacher, he worked with Saint Jane Frances Fremiot de Chantal for the foundation of the Visitation sisters. His feast day is on 24 January.

Francis of Assisi, Saint (1182–1226) Born John Bernardone in Assisi, Italy, and nicknamed Francis by his father, he enjoyed a carefree life of partying until taken prisoner in a local conflict. This helped to bring him to a deeper commitment to God, following the gospel in simplicity and poverty. Followers gathered, and an Order of brothers living in community according to the gospel was founded in 1209. Francis went to preach the gospel to the Saracens during a crusade, but without result. He encouraged Saint Clare of Assisi to found an order of nuns, while later he founded an Order of lay men and women penitents, known today as the Secular Franciscan Order. Never ordained priest, he was, in 1224, the first known person to receive the stigmata – the marks of the passion of Christ – in his body. His feast is celebrated on 4 October.

Fromm, Erich (1900–80) A German psychoanalyst who emigrated to the USA in 1932 to escape Nazism. He became professor of psychoanalysis at Yale University and published *The Fear of Freedom*, *The Sane Society*, *The Art of Loving* and *To Have or To Be*.

Gallican liturgy The liturgy in use in Gaul between the fourth and eighth centuries. Not a systematic or comprehensive body of rites, its origins are uncertain. Romanized versions of it survive today in Toledo (see Mozarabic liturgy) and Milan.

Gandhi, Mohandas Karamchand (1869–1948) Born in Porbandar, India, he trained for law in England. He settled in South Africa where he rallied opposition to discriminatory practices. Returning to India, he became leader of the National Congress, leading opposition to similar practices through peaceful non-cooperation and hunger strikes. He campaigned for social reform, religious tolerance, and, ultimately, for Indian independence, which came in 1948. Imprisoned several times for his beliefs, he was assassinated by a Hindu fanatic in 1948. Often known as 'Mahatma', a Sanskrit title meaning 'Great Soul'.

Gelasian Sacramentary Dating from the mid-eighth century, and originating in the north-east of France, it has no connection with any Gelasius, that name being a later addition assigned by the eighteenth-century Italian archivist, Lodovico Muratori. It probably is based on Roman and Gallican sources, now lost.

Gibbard, Mark An Anglican priest and member of the Community of the Resurrection at Mirfield, Yorkshire, England, he has written *Twentieth Century Men of Prayer* among other works.

Goodier, Alban M. R. (1869–1939) Born in Great Harwood, Lancashire, England, he joined the Jesuits in 1887, was ordained priest in 1903, and bishop in 1919. He resigned as bishop in 1926 and took up writing. Among his better-known works are *The Public Life of Our Lord Jesus Christ* (two vols), 1930 and *The Passion and Death of Our Lord Jesus Christ*, 1933.

Gregorian Sacramentary Beginning from Pope Saint Gregory I at the end of the sixth century, this Sacramentary went through a long and complex development, of which the principal parts were the work of Pope Adrian I, the *Hadrianum*, and additions by Alcuin, secretary to the Emperor Charlemagne. It continued in use until the eleventh century.

Gregory Nazianzus, Saint (*c.* 329–90) Born at Nazianzus in Turkey, Gregory travelled widely as a young man, being educated in Palestine and Greece before undertaking a life of solitude. He was ordained priest and bishop against his will and refused to take up his appointment. However, the effectiveness of his preaching against Arianism led to his being appointed Bishop of Constantinople in 380. His teaching on the divinity of Christ was accepted at the first council of Constantinople in 381. Continuing internal church conflicts led to his return to Nazianzus where he died. His writings, especially on the Trinity and on Christ, led to his being given the name of 'The Theologian'. His feast day is on 2 January.

Gregory of Nyssa, Saint (*c.* 330–95) Born in Caesarea, Cappadocia, Turkey, Gregory married, then became a priest, and finally Bishop of Nyssa in Armenia in 372. He was involved in the controversies against Arianism, but was exiled, in part as a result of his inexperience and tactlessness. After the death of his brother Saint Basil the Great, he became prominent, especially at the first council of Constantinople. Of his many writings, his *Catechetical Discourse* is best-known. He also wrote a biography of his sister, Saint Macrina. His feast is celebrated on 9 March.

Hadewijch of Brabant, Blessed Little is known of her life save that she was a Flemish noblewoman, probably from Brabant, Belgium, who lived before 1250. Her main literary activity was between 1230 and 1250: this consists of 11 'visions', 31 letters and 62 poems. Much of it deals with her mystical experiences which she claimed to be of the same nature as the beatific vision.

Hildegard of Bingen (1098–1179) Born at the court of Spandau, Germany, she began to experience visions at the age of six, became an anchorite with her aunt Jutta and took final vows at the age of 15. In 1136 she became the abbess of a community of Benedictine nuns at Disibode. She began to write of her mystical experiences and won the support of Saint Bernard and Pope Eugene III. In 1150 she formed a mixed community of monks and nuns near Bingen. In time she became, it is said, the first woman to write books: they included theology, philosophy, ethics, physiology, herbal treatments, music, poetry and biography, and she was the first woman to preach in public. She corresponded with popes, emperors, kings, abbots and mystics. In recent years there has been a revival of interest in her writings.

Ignatios of Latakia A Greek Orthodox bishop who took part in various assemblies of the World Council of Churches.

Ignatius of Antioch, Saint (died *c.* 107) He may have been a disciple of Saint John the Evangelist, probably became a Christian in adulthood and succeeded Saint Peter as Bishop of Antioch. In old age he was condemned to death and reputedly thrown to lions in a Roman amphitheatre. On his way there he wrote six letters to churches. Major themes of the letters are the reality of Christ's humanity, the need for unity among Christians, and respect for the bishop as the focus of unity. In style they are passionate and excited, characterized by strong faith and a joyful anticipation of martyrdom. His feast is celebrated on 17 October.

Ignatius Loyola, Saint (1491–1556) Iñigo de Recalde was born at Loyola, Spain; he spent his early life at the royal court and in the army. Injury in battle led to a more committed religious life, a pilgrimage to the Holy Land, and to the study of theology in Paris, where he was ordained priest. Companions gathered round him, and, with them, he later founded in Rome the Society of Jesus which pledged to undertake any work assigned by the pope. It became a pillar of the Counter-Reformation through education and missionary work. His *Spiritual Exercises* have become a standard workbook for retreatants everywhere. His feast is celebrated on 31 July.

Irenaeus, Saint (*c.* 140–*c.* 200) He was brought up by Saint Polycarp at Izmir, Turkey. By 177 he was a priest at Lyons, France, becoming bishop there later. Among his writings against heresy, especially Gnosticism, are the *Adversus Haereses*. There is a doubtful tradition that he died a martyr's death. His feast is celebrated on 28 June.

Isidore of Seville, Saint (*c.* 560–636) Little is known of his early life. Succeeding his brother Leander as Bishop of Seville about 600, he presided over many regional councils, of which the more important were those of Seville in 609 and Toledo in 633. These regulated the life of the church in Spain. He also promoted the monastic life and education, decreeing that there should be a cathedral school of the liberal arts in every diocese. Among his many writings are books of history, geography, astronomy, biography, theology, a compilation of church laws and a short encyclopaedia. Known as 'The Schoolmaster of the Middle Ages' he is credited with completing work on the Mozarabic liturgy and with converting the Visigoths, whose history he wrote. His feast is celebrated on 4 April.

Jerome, Saint (340–420) Born at Strido, Croatia, he studied at Rome and was later baptized. He began to lead an ascetic life and was ordained priest against his will. He travelled widely before returning to Rome, becoming secretary to Pope Damasus and beginning the task of revising and retranslating the Bible into Latin (the Vulgate), and of promoting the monastic life. An irascible man, given to extremes, he retired to Bethlehem where he continued writing on Scripture until his death. His feast is celebrated on 30 September.

John of the Cross, Saint (*c.* 1542–91) Juan de Yepes y Alvarez was born at Fontiveros, Spain. He became a Carmelite in 1563 and was persuaded by Saint Teresa of Avila to undertake a reform of his Order, a task which caused him great suffering and even imprisonment. His writings, *The Ascent of Mount Carmel, The Spiritual Canticle, The Dark Night of the Soul* and his poems, are classics of Christian spirituality. A doctor of the church, his feast is celebrated on 14 December.

John Paul II, Pope (1920–) Born Karol Wojtyla at Wadowice, Poland, he studied clandestinely for the priesthood during the German occupation of his country during the Second World War. He became bishop in 1958, attended the Second Vatican Council and was elected Pope in 1978, being the first non-Italian for 400 years. He played a significant part in ending Communist rule in central and eastern Europe. He has undertaken many pastoral visits to all continents and has written extensively on every aspect of church life.

Johnson, Samuel (1709–84) An Englishman, Dr Johnson was a lexicographer (a 'harmless drudge', in his own words), author and critic.

Julian of Norwich (1342–c. 1420) An anchoress who lived at the church of Saints Julian and Edward at Norwich, England. Almost nothing is known of her, not even her name; she may have been educated by local Benedictine nuns. She describes herself as 'a simple, unlearned creature' writing for 'the little and the simple'. She is best-known for her *Revelations*, an informal and conversational description of her mystical experiences, in which she speaks of God as mother. The influence of the Johannine writings is clear in her teaching on the divine indwelling, and of Saint Paul on her ideas on incorporation in Christ. The depth, joy and hopefulness of her writings show her to have been a person of real spiritual insight.

Khomiakov, Alexis (1804–60) Born in Moscow, he was a well-educated member of the land-owning class. Both radical and traditional, he became the outstanding lay theologian of the Russian Orthodox Church. He advocated intellectual freedom, the abolition of censorship and of serfdom, but believed firmly in Russian rural tradition in opposition to those who urged the adoption of western ideas. A key concept in his writings was *Sobornost*, an idea embracing freedom and diversity, individuality and community, sometimes translated as catholicity. He died on his estate of cholera.

Knox, John (*c.* 1505–72) Born in Scotland, he became a Catholic priest, but was converted to the Reformed faith. Captured in Scotland by French troops in 1547, he was sent to the galleys as a slave but was released after two years as a result of intervention by the British government. Returning to Britain he became a royal chaplain and helped to compile the Prayer Book. When Mary became queen he fled, and was sentenced to death in his absence. He spent some time with Calvin in Geneva, returned home in 1559 and was charged with treason in Scotland, but acquitted. Regarded as the leading figure of the Reformation in Scotland, he wrote a *History of the Reformation in Scotland* and *The First Blast of the Trumpet Against the Monstrous Regiment of Women*.

Lawrence of the Resurrection, Brother (1611–91) Born Nicholas Hermann in Lorraine, France, he spent 18 years in the army before joining the Discalced Carmelites. Never ordained, he spent 30 years as cook in a friary in Paris. He became blind in his later years and died with a reputation for holiness. His spiritual notes and letters were published after his death. He is best known as the author of *The Practice of the Presence of God*.

Leo I, Pope Saint (died 461) Born in Tuscany, Italy, he was sent to Gaul as a mediator by Emperor Valentinian while still a deacon. Elected pope in 440, he opposed various sects which threatened the unity of the church. He reorganized the administrative structure of the church, consolidating his own position, with his universal primacy recognized by Emperor Valentinian in 445. His 'Tome' on the incarnation of Christ was accepted by the Council of Chalcedon in 451 as the basis of its doctrine. He showed great courage at the time of the invasions by Attila the Hun and Genseric the Vandal. His sermons and letters are of lasting value so that he is regarded as one of the Fathers of the church, and is one of only two popes with the title of 'the Great'. His feast is celebrated on 10 November.

Leonine Sacramentary The earliest surviving book of Roman Mass formularies and ordination prayers, it dates from the first quarter of the seventh century. Its compiler is unknown. It consists of a random collection of Mass texts, grouped by month. Although the contents are Roman in origin, they were not composed for use in Rome. Nor is there any clear connection, except perhaps in style, with Pope Saint Leo I (440–61) who collected Mass texts. It is also known as the Sacramentary of Verona, where the original text is kept in a single manuscript.

Lewis, Clive Staples (1898–1963) Born in Belfast, Ireland, and known as Jack, he was educated at Oxford where he later became professor of medieval literature. Initially an atheist, he became a Christian in the Church of England in 1929, describing his conversion in *Surprised by Joy*. Apart from literary criticism, science fiction, and children's books he wrote many outstanding works of Christian exposition and apologetic which still attract a wide readership today.

Longlonde, John (1473–1547) Born at Henley-on-Thames, England, he was educated at Oxford and was appointed Bishop of Lincoln in 1521 by King Henry VIII. He persecuted the Lollards, and was a judge on the court which heard Henry's divorce case. He supported royal supremacy over the church though it is said that he later regretted his involvement in the divorce. The benedictional which bears his name was prepared for him by an unknown compiler and was printed in 1528. His name is also given as Longland and Longlande.

Lubac, Henri de (1896–1991) Born in France, he joined the Jesuits in 1913. Though censured by the Holy Office, he went on to become one of the leading theologians of Vatican II and the post-conciliar period. He was created cardinal in 1983.

Macdonald, George (1824–1905) A Scottish novelist and writer of children's books, his mystical insights inspired Chesterton, Tolkien and C. S. Lewis.

Magdalen, Pontifical of An eleventh-century pontifical. (See *Pontifical*)

Main, John (1926–82) Born in London, England, of Irish parents he was in turn a journalist, soldier, barrister and monk. He lectured in law at Trinity College, Dublin, before joining the Benedictines in 1959. Renowned for his spiritual writings, especially on meditation, he was the inspiration for the founding of the World Community for Christian Meditation which has about 1000 groups in some 40 countries. Among his best-known works are *Word Into Silence*, *Moment of Christ* and *The Present Christ*.

Makarios the Great, Saint (*c.* 300–*c.* 390) Born in Upper Egypt, he began work as a camel-driver before becoming a monk and a priest in the desert of Skete (the Wadi al-Natrun). He was noted for his asceticism, shrewdness and gentleness. Many of his sayings are recorded in *The Sayings of the Desert Fathers*. His feast is celebrated in the eastern churches on 19 January.

Mandela, Nelson (1918–) Born near Umbata, South Africa, he trained as a lawyer. Becoming involved in the work of the African National Congress, he was charged with treason in 1961, but acquitted. Rearrested in 1964 he was sentenced to life imprisonment for sabotage and plotting to overthrow the government. Released from prison in 1990, he was elected president of the ANC the following year and began negotiations with the de Klerk government about a new constitutional order in South Africa. He was awarded the Nobel Peace Prize in 1993 and was elected president in 1994. His autobiography, *Long Walk to Freedom*, is widely acclaimed.

Margaret Mary Alacoque, Saint (1647–90) Born in Burgundy, France, she joined the Visitation nuns in 1671. She had a series of mystical experiences, centred around the Sacred Heart of Jesus, and stressing God's love for humanity, in contrast to the prevailing rigorism which derived from the writings of Bishop Cornelius Jansens, known as Jansenism. She experienced much misunderstanding and opposition, and was tempted to despair, although she was supported by her confessor, Blessed Claude de la Colombière. She died at Paray-le-Monial, and her feast is celebrated on 16 October.

Mark, the liturgy of Saint The title given to the liturgical rites of the Church of Alexandria, Egypt, and attributed to Saint Mark the Evangelist. Before the Council of Chalcedon in 541, its language was Greek. After Chalcedon, Greek was used only by the Melchites, while the Copts and Ethiopians used Coptic and Ge'ez. It has not been used in Greek since the twelfth century. The earliest known fragments are a fourth-century papyrus.

Maronite Church, the One of the Catholic eastern churches, its members are found mainly in the Lebanon, Syria and, especially in recent years, in the United States. Claiming origin from Saint Maron (350–433), they follow the liturgy of Saint James in the Aramaic language. In full communion with Rome since the fifth Lateran Council (1512–17), they are now almost completely Romanized.

Mechthild of Magdeburg (*c.* 1209–82) Born in Saxony, Germany, she became a Béguin nun about 1230 and lived a life of prayer and austerity for some 40 years. Her criticisms of the clergy and her claim to have received supernatural favours brought her much opposition in later years. Her principal work, *The Flowing Forth of the Light of the Godhead*, which uses the image of God as the Light, has been published in English; it is a collection of poems, love songs, allegories, visions, moral admonitions and reflections. She died at Helfta. She is sometimes confused with her contemporary, Saint Mechthild of Helfta, with whom she spent the last years of her life while suffering from blindness.

Melanchton, Philip (1497–1560) Born at Bretten, in Baden, Germany, he was educated at Heidelberg and Tübingen, where he became a lecturer. He became professor of Greek at Wittenberg in 1518, and met Luther there. Gradually becoming the theologian of the Reformation, he defended the Protestant cause in the Augsburg Confession in 1530, and at Worms in 1557. He was the founder of higher education for Protestants in Germany.

Merton, Thomas (1915–68) Born in France, grew up in France and England. He was educated at Cambridge in England and at Colombia University in the United States. He underwent a religious conversion leading to his joining the Cistercians and becoming a priest. His many writings on spirituality attracted a wide readership in the English-speaking world. *The Seven Storey Mountain*, published in 1946, is his autobiography. During the Vietnam war, he took a strongly anti-war stance. He also pursued dialogue with other religions, particularly Buddhism. He died in Bangkok.

Mozarabic liturgy The origin of the term 'Mozarabic' is unclear. It describes the liturgy used in Iberia from the sixth to the eleventh centuries; also known as the Gothic liturgy since it arose during the Visigothic kingdom in Spain. Its centre was Toledo, where it is still in use, and its principal architect was Saint Isidore of Seville. Of a common origin and almost identical construction to the Gallican liturgy.

Newman, John Henry (1801–90) Born in London, England, Newman was ordained in the Church of England in 1824. He wrote a series of tracts called *Tracts for the Times*, which gave rise to the Oxford Movement. He became a Catholic in 1845, and was made cardinal in 1879. In 1854–58 he was rector of a projected Catholic University of Dublin, Ireland. Among his best-known writings are his autobiography, the *Apologia pro Vita Sua*, and the *Grammar of Assent*, an analysis of the nature of belief.

Nicene Creed A statement of the basic teachings of the Christian faith drawn up at the general council of Nicaea in 325, and revised at the first council of Constantinople in 381. In 1014 it was adopted for use at Mass. It is this creed which is said in the Sunday Eucharist of many mainline Christian churches.

Nicholas of Cusa (1401–64) German-born Bishop of Brixen in the Tyrol, a philosopher, he is seen as being involved in the transition from Scholasticism to modern philosophy. In his best-known work, *De docta Ignorantia* (Of Learned Ignorance), he argued that God completely transcends human mental categories and dualisms, and is therefore above all knowledge, even the best of which is merely learned ignorance. In cosmology he broke with tradition by asserting that the universe is boundless.

Obbard, Elizabeth Ruth An American Carmelite nun, she has written *A Retreat with Thérèse of Lisieux: Loving Our Way to Holiness*.

Ó Callanáin, Pádraig A nineteenth-century Irish poet who lived in Galway, Ireland.

O'Collins, Gerald Professor of Theology at the Gregorian University in Rome and the author of many books.

Ó Conaill, Seán A retired teacher who lives in Coleraine, Derry, Ireland, and contributes to religious journals. Author of *Scattering the Proud: Christianity Beyond 2000*, The Columba Press, Dublin, 1999.

Orthodox The name derives from the Greek *orthos*, true, and *doxa*, doctrine. The Orthodox churches are national churches of Eastern Europe, which, while possessing valid sacraments, have been separated from communion with the pope since the ninth century. Also called Byzantine, or eastern, churches.

Pascal, Blaise (1623–62) Born at Clermond-Ferrand, France, Pascal was a philosopher, mathematician and Christian apologist. He contributed to the development of calculus and hydraulics, and invented and sold several elementary calculators, as well as designing a public transport system for Paris which was inaugurated in 1662. His principal apologetic work was his *Pensées* (Thoughts), which was still incomplete when he died.

Patrick, Saint (*c.* 385–461) Born in the west of Britain, he was brought up a Christian before being captured and taken to Ireland as a slave. He escaped, went to France and was ordained bishop about 432. Pope Celestine I sent him to bring the faith to the Christians of Ireland as successor to Palladius. Working with the tribal chiefs, he achieved substantial success, founding his principal see at Armagh. Among the writings attributed to him, the *Confession* and the *Letter to Coroticus*, both warm human documents, are probably authentically his. His feast is celebrated on 17 March.

Paul VI, Pope (1897–1978) Born Giovanni Battista Montini near Brescia, Italy, he spent most of his life in the Vatican, except for five years from 1958 to 1963 as Archbishop of Milan. Elected pope in 1963, his great work was the implementation of the decisions of the Second Vatican Council (1962–65).

Péguy, Charles Pierre (1873–1914) A French Catholic socialist poet and writer on political questions.

Philaret of Moscow, Metropolitan (1782–1867) Vasili Mikhailovich Drozdov was born near Moscow, Russia, the son of a Russian Orthodox priest. He became a monk with the name of Philaret in 1808, and was ordained priest in 1809. He became rector of a seminary, bishop, and then metropolitan of Moscow. In the face of much opposition, he had the Bible translated into Russian and the catechism revised; it was subsequently translated into several languages. He tried to reunite the Ukrainian Catholics with the Orthodox Church, and was hostile to the Catholic Church and especially the pope. He advocated the abolition of serfdom in Russia.

Pius XI, Pope (1857–1939) Born Achille Ratti near Milan, Italy, he became pope in 1922. He normalized the relationship between the Holy See and Italy by the Lateran Treaty of 1929, was a vigorous promoter of missionary work, especially of the need for a local clergy, and opposed totalitarianism, writing encyclical letters against fascism (*Non abbiamo bisogno*), Nazism (*Mit brennender Sorge*) and Communism (*Divini Redemptoris*).

Pontifical A book of liturgical texts containing the rites of ordinations and consecrations reserved to a bishop. The first Roman pontifical was published in 1485.

Powell, John An American priest of the Society of Jesus, he writes widely on spirituality, combining insights from psychology. Works include *The Christian Vision*, and *Fully Human, Fully Divine*.

Processional A liturgical book containing the order to be followed in a procession; in medieval times, a book with information on a local church.

Proust, Marcel (1871–1922) Born at Auteuil, France, he became a novelist and critic. His best-known work was *A la recherche du temps perdu*, an autobiographical series of novels depicting life in France at the end of the nineteenth century.

Psalter The Old Testament collection of 150 psalms, or a book containing the same, arranged for the recitation of the Divine Office individually or chorally.

Quiercy, Councils of A series of regional councils held in the eighth and ninth centuries at the seat of the Frankish kings near Noyon, France. In 853, in opposition to the teaching of Gottschalk, the council affirmed that God wills the salvation of all people and that Christ died for the sins of all humanity.

Quoist, Michel (1918–) A French diocesan priest, based at Le Havre, his spiritual writings, especially *Prayers of Life*, enjoyed great popularity both in France and in English-speaking countries in the 1960s. Recently published: *New Prayers*.

Rahner, Karl (1904–84) Born in Germany, he joined the Jesuits and became one of the leading theologians at Vatican II and in the postconciliar period. His voluminous writings include a number of works of spirituality, including *The Love of Jesus and the Love of Neighbour*.

137

Réamonn, Seán Mac Irish journalist, broadcaster and writer. A prominent layman in the Irish Catholic Church.

Redemptorists The Congregation of the Most Holy Redeemer (CSsR), a Catholic religious congregation founded by Saint Alphonsus Liguori in 1732.

Rice, Blessed Edmund Ignatius (1762–1844) Born in Callan, Kilkenny, Ireland, into a wealthy family, Edmund married in 1785. However, his wife died just four years later and their only child was handicapped. From his earliest years he had cared for poor children, feeding and teaching them. In 1802 he began his first school; other men joined him and the Congregation of Christian Brothers, and later Presentation Brothers, came into being. Today, they have schools of all kinds on five continents. He was declared Blessed in 1996.

Ritual A book containing the texts of liturgical rites.

Rolheiser, Ronald A Canadian priest, a member of the Oblates of Mary Immaculate, he writes frequently on spiritual matters in books and newspapers, and is engaged in retreat work.

Roman Of the Roman Catholic Church.

Ruth, Sister A member of the Sisters of the Love of God community of Anglican nuns in Oxford, England.

Ruysbroeck, Blessed Jan van (1293–1381) He was born at Ruysbroeck, near Brussels, Belgium. Educated by an uncle who was a canon of the cathedral chapter, he was ordained priest in 1317. But in 1343, with two companions, he withdrew to a lonely valley in search of solitude, spending the rest of his life in prayer, writing, and giving spiritual counsel. In 1350, the three became Canons of Saint Augustine. Jan was widely known for his spirituality, which reveals something of Eckhart's influence; among those who visited him was Johannes Tauler, who, along with Meister Eckhart and Henry Suso, was one of the famous Rhineland school of mystical preachers and teachers. His writings, in the Brabant dialect of Flemish, reached a wide audience in his own country. Some have been translated into English under the titles *The Sparkling Stone* and *The Adornment of the Spiritual Marriage*. Known in his lifetime as 'Jan the Admirable', he was beatified in 1908.

Sacramentary A sacramentary is a book containing the rites of the sacraments, including the rite of celebrating Mass. The term is sometimes used more narrowly as a synonym for a Missal. In the western tradition, some of the best-known are the Celtic, Franciscan, Gallican, Gelasian, Gregorian, Leonine, Milanese, Mozarabic and Roman.

Sarum The word derives from Sarisburia, the Latin name for Salisbury, England, one of the principal English episcopal sees. Beginning with missionaries sent to England by Pope Saint Gregory I in 596 under Saint Augustine of Canterbury, a musical tradition developed which, with Gallican and Norman French influences after 1066, lasted until the Reformation. It was revived by Anglican scholars in the nineteenth century. Other liturgical texts, such as the Primer, claim their origin from Salisbury.

Scottish Psalter The first version of the Scottish Psalter, or book of psalms, influenced by that of Geneva, was produced in 1564 by Protestant groups who had left Britain because of religious persecution. There were several later editions, of which that of 1650 exchanged artistic vitality for practical usefulness, and reduced the metrical patterns of earlier editions to the monotony of the English common metre.

Seraphim of Sarov, Saint (1759–1833) A teacher, lover of nature and mystic, this monk and priest spent some 20 years in solitude before becoming a *staretz*, or spiritual guide, visited daily by large numbers of pilgrims from all parts of Russia. His feast is celebrated in the Russian Orthodox Church on 2 January.

Shakespeare, William (1564–1616) Born in Stratford-upon-Avon, England, a dramatist, actor and poet, he was the author of some 37 plays.

Shaw, Gilbert Began his career as a barrister, then became a clergyman in the Church of England. His *Pilgrim's Book of Prayers* was first published in 1945. Active in retreat work, he was warden of the Sisters of the Love of God in Oxford from 1964 until his death in 1967.

Sobrino, Jon A contemporary South American liberation theologian, he has written and lectured widely.

Society of Saint Francis A religious order of Anglican Franciscans, founded in England, now widespread in the English-speaking world.

Steindl-Ross, David A contemporary monk of the Russian Orthodox Church living in the USA, he writes on spirituality (*A Listening Heart*, among others) and has edited some spiritual works by classical authors.

Sulivan, Jean (1913–80) The pseudonym of a French diocesan priest whose spiritual journal has been published in English under the title *Morning Light*. He has also written *The Sea Remains* and *Eternity my Beloved*. He was killed in a road accident.

Symeon the new theologian, Saint (949–1022) A mystical theologian and poet, he was the abbot of the monastery of Saint Mamas in Constantinople. A central image in his writings is that of God as the Light.

Syrian liturgy Originally the rite of the Church of Antioch, Syria, dating from the fourth century, it was written in Greek; in later centuries Syriac was used, and Arabic in modern times. The rite is used today by Jacobites and Catholics in Syria and Lebanon. One of its features is the Liturgy of Saint James, which has 64 Eucharistic Prayers.

Temple, William (1884–1944) An English churchman, he became Archbishop of Canterbury in 1942. His principal concerns were for Christian unity and for living the Christian faith in social life.

Teresa of Avila, Saint (1515–82) Born in Spain, she joined the Carmelites in her home town, where she led a relaxed and comfortable life. However, in 1562 she led a reform movement based on a return to the authentic tradition of Carmel. Supported by Saint Peter of Alcántara and working with Saint John of the Cross, she set up 16 houses of the reform, despite ill-health, intense opposition and a lack of resources. Her writings, especially her *Life*, *The Interior Castle* and *The Way of Perfection*, are among the great classics of Christian spirituality. They combine spiritual insight, humour, kindness and hard-headed realism. She was declared a doctor of the church in 1970 by Pope Paul VI and her feast is celebrated on 15 October.

Teresa of Calcutta, Mother (1910–97) Born Agnes Gonxha Bojaxhiu in Skopje, Macedonia and educated in Ireland, she joined the Loreto Sisters and taught in their schools in India. Her 'second vocation', to serve 'the poorest of the poor' led her to live among, and work with, destitute people in Calcutta. In 1948 she founded the Missionaries of Charity, now a world-wide congregation of Sisters, engaging in similar work. She was awarded the Nobel Peace Prize in 1979.

Thérèse of Lisieux, Saint (1873–97) Born in Alençon, France, she joined the Carmelite nuns while still only 15, having made a personal appeal to Pope Leo XIII. Nine years later she died of tuberculosis, leaving behind her autobiography and letters which, when purged of the 'editorial' work of her Sisters, reveal a person who grew enormously in a short time, learning how the apparently insignificant things in life can be invested with great value, how to live with the apparent absence of God, and to accept that our love for God is a gift rather than an achievement. Patroness of the foreign missions and of Russia, she was declared a doctor of the church by Pope John Paul II. Her feast is celebrated on 1 October.

Thomas à Kempis (*c.* 1379–1471) Born at Kempen, near Düsseldorf, Germany, he joined a community of Augustinian canons in 1399, and was ordained priest in 1413. He spent his life as a copyist of manuscripts and in writing chronicles and devotional works, of which the best-known is the *Imitation of Christ*. He is considered the outstanding exponent of the *devotio moderna* (a spiritual movement which was characterized by its moralism, asceticism and stress on Scripture and withdrawal from the world). He moved to Zwolle in the Netherlands three years before his death.

Thomas Aquinas, Saint (1225–74) Born in Aquino, Italy, he studied at Monte Cassino and Paris, and at Cologne under Saint Albert the Great. A Dominican friar, he was perhaps the greatest philosopher and theologian of the church, and has left a large body of writings. His principal works are the *Summa contra Gentiles* and the *Summa Theologica*; he has also left some religious poems, especially the Office for *Corpus Christi*.

Thomas More, Saint (1477–1535) Born in London, England, he received a classical education and became a lawyer. Married with four children, he became a favourite of King Henry VIII, becoming Lord Chancellor (prime minister) in 1529, but resigned three years later because of disagreement with the king about the latter's marriage and claim to supremacy over the church. He spent the years of his retirement engaged in writing. In 1535 he was charged with treason, condemned and beheaded. His feast is celebrated on 22 June along with Saint John Fisher, another English martyr of the Reformation.

Vanier, Jean The founder of the l'Arche and Faith and Light communities, which offer people with mental disabilities and those who share their lives a place where they can belong and grow. He is the author of many books, including *The Broken Body: Journey to Wholeness*.

Voillaume, René For a time was the superior of the Little Brothers of Jesus founded by Charles de Foucauld. Among his writings is *Seeds of the Desert*.

Ware, Kallistos A fellow of Pembroke College, Oxford, and a bishop of the Orthodox Church, he has written on spirituality. Among his writings are *The Power of the Name*, a study of the Jesus Prayer.

Way of a Pilgrim, The An anonymous work of spirituality, written in Russia, probably between 1853 and 1861. The second part, *The Pilgrim Continues His Way*, was probably written by another author.

Weimarischer Gesangbuch A Lutheran hymnal produced at Weimar, Germany, in 1873.

Whitford, Richard An English Bridgettine monk and spiritual writer of the sixteenth century.

Wilde, Oscar (1854–1900) Born in Ireland and educated in Oxford, his witty conversation made him the darling of London society. A novelist, poet and playwright, he was imprisoned in 1895 for a homosexual affair with Lord Alfred Douglas, and went into exile in France after his release in 1897. His later writings, especially *The Ballad of Reading Gaol*, have a theme of repentance and forgiveness.

William of Saint Thierry (1085–1148) Born at Liège, Belgium, William joined the Benedictines at Reims. Between 1116 and 1118 he formed a lasting friendship with Saint Bernard of Clairvaux. In 1135, seeking a more contemplative life, he joined the Cistercians at Signy. His very substantial writings on mystical theology and spirituality focus on the Trinity and draw their inspiration from Scripture and, especially, the writings of the Fathers.

DOCUMENTS OF THE SECOND VATICAN COUNCIL (VATICAN II, 1962–65)

Ad Gentes The decree on the church's missionary activity.

Apostolicam Actuositatem The decree on the apostolate of laypeople.

Christus Dominus The decree on the pastoral office of bishops.

Dei Verbum The dogmatic constitution on divine revelation.

Dignitatis Humanae The declaration on religious liberty.

Gaudium et Spes The pastoral constitution on the church in the modern world.

Gravissimum Educationis The declaration on Christian education.

Inter Mirifica The decree on the instruments of social communication.

Lumen Gentium The dogmatic constitution on the church.

Nostra Aetate The declaration on the church's relationship with non-Christian religions.

Optatam Totius The decree on the training of priests.

Orientalium Ecclesiarum The decree on the Catholic eastern churches.

Perfectae Caritatis The decree on the renewal and adaptation of the religious life.

Presbyterorum Ordinis The decree on the life and ministry of priests.

Sacrosanctum Concilium The constitution on the liturgy.

Unitatis Redintegratio The decree on ecumenism.

Note

The term 'Post-Vatican II documents' in this book refers to those documents, issued after the Second Vatican Council (1962–65), which were intended to implement its decisions.

COMMON PRAYERS

The Sign of the Cross

In the name of the Father, and of the Son, and of the Holy Spirit. Amen.

Our Father

Our Father, who art in heaven,
hallowed be thy name;
thy kingdom come;
thy will be done on earth as it is in heaven.
Give us this day our daily bread;
and forgive us our trespasses
as we forgive those who trespass against us;
and lead us not into temptation,
but deliver us from evil. Amen.

Hail, Mary

Hail, Mary, full of grace, the Lord is with you!
Blessed are you among women,
and blessed is the fruit of your womb, Jesus.
Holy Mary, Mother of God, pray for us sinners
now and at the hour of our death. Amen.

Glory

Glory be to the Father,
and to the Son,
and to the Holy Spirit,
as it was in the beginning,
is now, and ever shall be,
world without end. Amen.

The Apostles' Creed

I believe in God, the Father almighty, Creator of heaven and earth.

I believe in Jesus Christ, his only Son, our Lord.
He was conceived by the power of the Holy Spirit
and born of the Virgin Mary.
He suffered under Pontius Pilate,

was crucified, died, and was buried.
He descended to the dead.
On the third day he rose again.
He ascended into heaven,
and is seated at the right hand of the Father.
He will come again to judge the living and the dead.

I believe in the Holy Spirit,
the holy catholic church,
the communion of saints,
the forgiveness of sins,
the resurrection of the body,
and the life everlasting. Amen.

Glory to God

Glory to God in the highest,
and peace to his people on earth.

Lord God, heavenly King,
Almighty God and Father,
we worship you, we give you thanks,
we praise you for your glory.

Lord Jesus Christ, only Son of the Father,
Lord God, Lamb of God,
You take away the sin of the world:
have mercy on us;
you are seated at the right hand of the Father:
receive our prayer.

For you alone are the Holy One,
You alone are the Lord,
You alone are the Most High,
Jesus Christ,
with the Holy Spirit,
in the glory of God the Father. Amen.

An act of sorrow

My God, I thank you for loving me.
I am sorry for all my sins,
for not loving others and for not loving you.
Help me to live like Jesus lived,
and not sin again. Amen.

The Nicene Creed

We believe in one God,
the Father, the Almighty,
maker of heaven and earth,
of all that is, seen and unseen.

We believe in one Lord, Jesus Christ,
the only Son of God,
eternally begotten of the Father,
God from God, Light from Light,
true God from true God,
begotten, not made, of one Being with the Father.
Through him all things were made.
For us and for our salvation
he came down from heaven:
was incarnate of the Holy Spirit
and the Virgin Mary, and was made man.
For our sake he was crucified under Pontius Pilate;
he suffered, died, and was buried.
On the third day he rose again
in accordance with the Scriptures;
he ascended into heaven
and is seated at the right hand of the Father.
He will come again in glory to judge the living and the dead,
and his kingdom will have no end.

We believe in the Holy Spirit, the Lord, the giver of life,
who proceeds from the Father and the Son.
With the Father and the Son he is worshipped and glorified.
He has spoken through the prophets.
We believe in one holy catholic and apostolic church.
We acknowledge one baptism for the forgiveness of sins.
We look for the resurrection of the dead,
and the life of the world to come. Amen.